The World Wars

THE SECOND WORLD WAR

Edited by Stewart Ross
from an original text by
Michel Pierre and Annette Wieviorka
English translation by Christopher Sharp
Picture research by Martine Mairal

Wayland

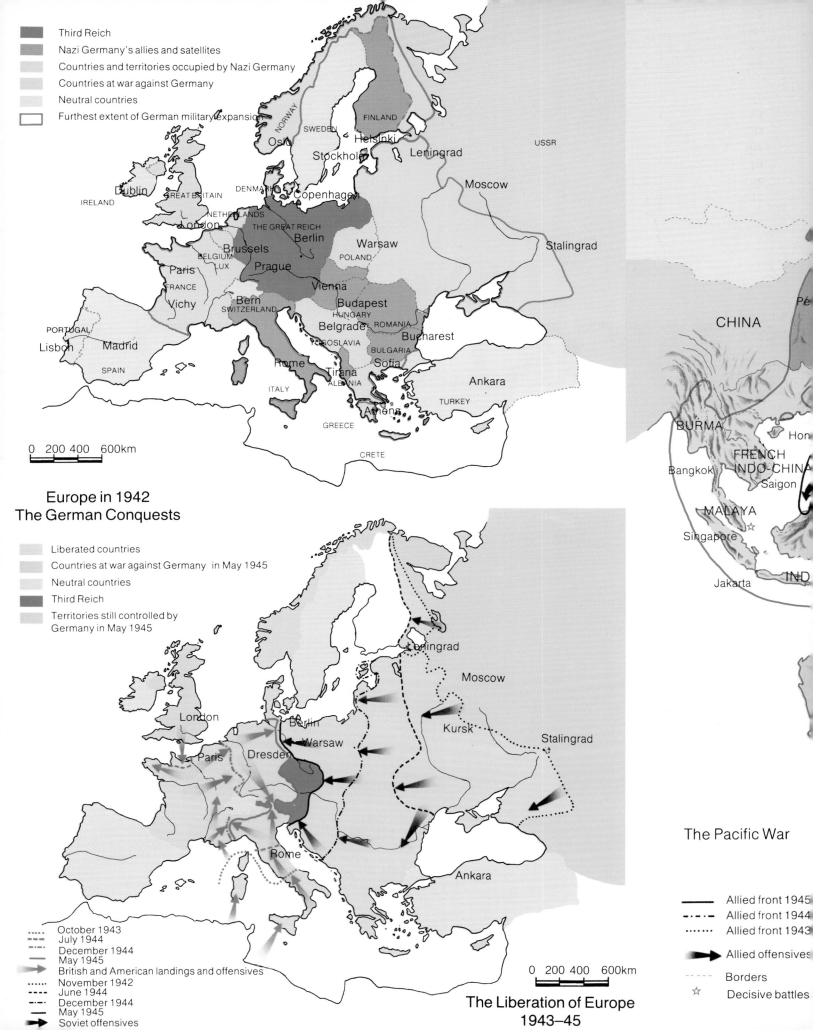

Europe in 1942
The German Conquests

Third Reich
Nazi Germany's allies and satellites
Countries and territories occupied by Nazi Germany
Countries at war against Germany
Neutral countries
Furthest extent of German military expansion

NORWAY
Oslo
SWEDEN
Stockholm
FINLAND
Helsinki
Leningrad
USSR
Moscow

IRELAND
Dublin
GREAT BRITAIN
London
DENMARK
Copenhagen
NETHERLANDS
BELGIUM
LUX
THE GREAT REICH
Berlin
Brussels
Prague
Warsaw
POLAND
Stalingrad

Paris
FRANCE
Vichy
Bern
SWITZERLAND
Vienna
Budapest
HUNGARY
ROMANIA
Bucharest

PORTUGAL
Lisbon
Madrid
SPAIN
Rome
Belgrade
YUGOSLAVIA
BULGARIA
Sofia
Ankara

ITALY
Tirana
ALBANIA
Athens
GREECE
TURKEY

CRETE

0 200 400 600km

CHINA

BURMA
Hon
FRENCH
INDO-CHINA
Bangkok
Saigon
MALAYA
Singapore
IND
Jakarta

Liberated countries
Countries at war against Germany in May 1945
Neutral countries
Third Reich
Territories still controlled by Germany in May 1945

Leningrad
Moscow
London
Berlin
Warsaw
Dresden
Kursk
Stalingrad
Paris
Rome
Ankara

.... October 1943
– – – July 1944
–·–·– December 1944
——— May 1945
➤ British and American landings and offensives
.... November 1942
– – – June 1944
–·–·– December 1944
——— May 1945
➤ Soviet offensives

The Liberation of Europe
1943–45

0 200 400 600km

The Pacific War

——— Allied front 1945
–·–·– Allied front 1944
.... Allied front 1943
➤ Allied offensives
– – – Borders
☆ Decisive battles

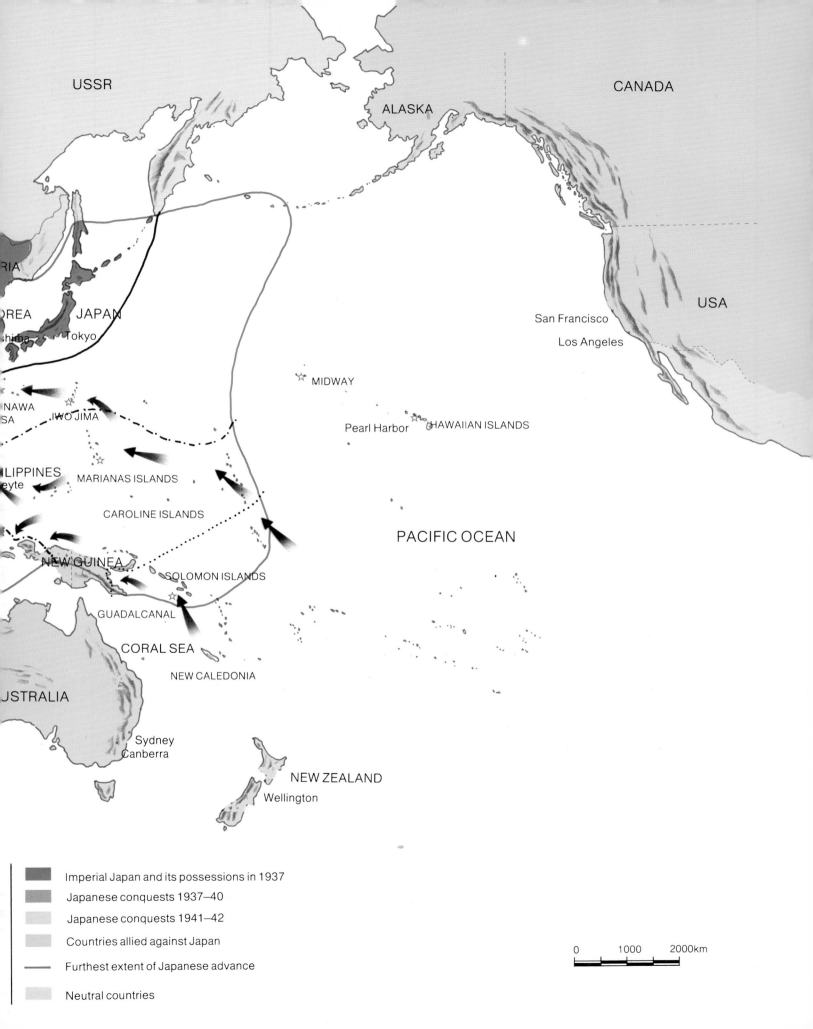

USSR

ALASKA

CANADA

RIA

KOREA JAPAN

hima Tokyo

USA

San Francisco

Los Angeles

MIDWAY

NAWA
SA

IWO JIMA

Pearl Harbor HAWAIIAN ISLANDS

LIPPINES
eyte

MARIANAS ISLANDS

CAROLINE ISLANDS

PACIFIC OCEAN

NEW GUINEA

SOLOMON ISLANDS

GUADALCANAL

CORAL SEA

NEW CALEDONIA

USTRALIA

Sydney
Canberra

NEW ZEALAND

Wellington

Imperial Japan and its possessions in 1937

Japanese conquests 1937–40

Japanese conquests 1941–42

Countries allied against Japan

Furthest extent of Japanese advance

Neutral countries

0   1000   2000km

© 1985 Casterman, originally published in French under the title *Les Jours de l'Histoire: La Seconde Guerre Mondiale*.

© 1987 English text, Silver Burdett Press. Published pursuant to an agreement with Casterman, Paris.

All Rights Reserved.

© This edition Wayland (Publishers) Ltd

First published in the UK in 1989 by
Wayland (Publishers) Ltd
61 Western Road,
Hove, East Sussex BN3 1DU

British Library Cataloguing in Publication Data
Pierre, Michel *1946*–
The Second World War.—(The World Wars).
1. World War 2.
I Title.   II Wieviorka, Annette.
III Ross Stewart. IV Series. V *English*
940.5J

ISBN 185210 797 9

Picture Credits

MAGNUM: 6/CDJC: 40 *b*, 42/COLL. PART BY CASTERMAN: 9 *t*, 13, 16 *t*, 18 *t*, 18 *t*, 26, 36 *b*, 37, 38 *t*, 45 *t*, 53 *t*/EDIMEDIA: 9 *b*, 14 (cartoon by Derzo and Kelen), 40 *t*, 63 *b*, 66/PHOTOTHEQUE FRANCE-USSR: 10, 28 *t*, 30, 31 *b*, 46 *t*, *b*, 47 col, 48, 49, 61 *b*, 65, 69/ROGER-VIOLLET: 11 *b*, 13 *t*, 14 *b*, 33/B.D.I.C. Musée des 2 guerres mondiales: 15 (by Trampus), 18 *b* (by Hoffman, D.R.), 25 *t* (by Thérèse Bonney), 25 *b* (by Nora), 28 *b* (by Hoffman, D.R.), 29 *t* (by Weltbild, D.R.), 29 *b* (Presse bild zentrale, D.R.), 34–35, 36 *t*, 38 *b* (by Scherl, D.R.), 38–39 *b* (F.F.L., D.R.), 39 (by Scherl, D.R.), 41 *b*, 43, 44 *b*, 45 *b* (F.F.L., D.R.), 48–49 (Planet News, D.R.), 50, 52 (Associated Press, D.R.), 53 *b* (Information), 54 *b*, 55 *b*,56, 5859 *b* (Presse liberation, D.R.), 59 *t* (Coll. part Lefrançois), 60 *t* (by Scherl, D.R.)/INVALIDES, Musée des 2 guerres mondiales: 22, 24, 31 *t*, 32, 39 *t*, 41 *t*, 47 *t*, 51 *t*, *b*, 61 *t*/RAPHO: 27 *b*/DRESDEN VERLAG: 64/KEYSTONE: 68.

FRONT COVER: Photo Thérèse Bonney, BDIC, Musée des 2 guerres mondiales/BACK COVER: BDIC, Musée des 2 guerres mondiales (E.C.P.A., D.R.).

Contents

Memories of the Great War

In 1938, Europe was still living with the memory of the Great War (the First World War) of 1914–18. No one could forget the bloodshed that had cost the lives of eight million men. The countries that were victorious in this first world conflict, including Britain, France, and the USA, expected never to hear the sound of gunfire again. For them 11 November, the anniversary of the armistice of 1918, was a day of glory. But in some of the defeated countries, Germany and Austria for example, there were those who dreamed of revenge. The Nazis, who had been ruling Germany for the past five years, were foremost among them.

All over Europe, in large towns and tiny villages, 11 November was marked with ceremonies of remembrance. In Britain, for example, millions observed two minutes silence before 11 a.m. They stood quietly grieving, recalling the faces of those who had perished in the 'war to end all wars'. There was not a community of any kind – town, school or club – that did not have its own sad list of young men who had died in some foreign field.

At 11 a.m. bugles sounded the last post. The eyes of the war veterans filled with tears as they remembered the horror of trenches, explosions, bullet-ridden bodies, and flying shrapnel. Their only desire was never to relive such a war. They prayed fervently that it would never happen again.

Almost everyone hoped that the treaty signed in 1919 at Versailles would guarantee lasting peace. They wanted to believe that the countries created after the war, such as Yugoslavia, Czechoslovakia and Poland, would remain stable nations. People also placed hope in the Geneva-based League of Nations, which represented fifty-two countries. Its delegates were charged with settling tensions and conflicts peacefully.

However, the 1930s had begun with worrying news. An economic crisis had developed in the United States and spread to the rest of the world. It prepared the way for Adolf Hitler's rise to power in Germany in 1933 and helped Japan's warlike ambitions in Asia.

Most citizens of the western democracies, however, thought that the main goal of their governments, should be to maintain peace at all costs. They were not concerned with the warlike speeches given by Hitler, or by Benito Mussolini, who had been the Italian dictator in power since 1922. France, for example, was a peaceful country. It was tired of war and largely made up of old people. The hundreds of thousands of young men killed during the war were irreplaceable. Among those remaining, in 1935 the number of deaths exceeded that of births. This was exceptional in peacetime.

Neither Britain nor France was prepared for another war. Faced with the disastrous economic slump of the early 1930s, their governments had cut defence expenditure. This meant fewer warplanes, smaller armies and weaker navies. Disillusionment with war was just as strong in the USA, where the Senate had even refused to ratify the Treaty of Versailles, thereby keeping the USA out of the League of Nations. When the great depression hit, Americans lost all interest in the affairs of the rest of the world as they struggled to come to terms with unaccustomed poverty.

Many French and British politicians now recognized that the Treaty of Versailles had been a mistake. It had forced the Germans to pay impossible reparations, thus ruining their already war-torn economy. They were made to accept full responsibility for the outbreak of the Great War, and their country had been divided up, German-speaking peoples finding themselves living in Poland, Czechoslovakia and other neighbouring countries. By the 1930s western leaders felt guilt at their predecessors' behaviour and they came to recognize some justification in the demands of Hitler and Mussolini. Many still believed that Nazi Germany did not pose a real threat to peace in the world. Hitler was soon to prove them wrong.

'For Liberty and the Homeland' was the message of a German poster condemning the Treaty of Versailles. (This was the treaty drawn up in 1919 after the First World War.) Hitler was able to play on the feelings of the German people, who had never accepted the clauses of a treaty they considered unfair and humiliating.

Opposite: In 1938, France had 5,200,000 war veterans from the Great War. Among them, 300,000 were disabled, blind, or permanently affected by mustard gas. Their bodies were scarred by a war which sacrificed a whole generation. War benefits paid by the State to these veterans or their widows and orphans placed a heavy burden on the budget of a country whose population was at near zero growth.

Germany Under the Swastika

The sign reads: 'Germans defend yourselves! Don't buy from Jews!' On 1 April 1934, Hitler's propaganda minister, Joseph Goebbels, began a campaign to boycott Jewish stores, and entrusted the SA (Assault Sections) with the task. These 'brown shirts', as they were called, were noted for their violence against Jews and political opponents. Created by Hitler in 1921, the SA totalled three million men in 1934. The power of this 'brown' army, which had its own police, prisons, and training camps, was such that Hitler, worried about this state within a state, had its leaders assassinated during the 'Night of the Long Knives' (June 1934).

At three o'clock in the morning on 10 November 1938, all was quiet in Germany. Suddenly in Berlin, Hamburg, Leipzig, and in most of the country's other cities, groups of SS (security forces), dressed in civilian clothes and armed with hammers, axes, and clubs burst into flats inhabited by Jewish people. The dwellings were ransacked and those in them beaten up. Thirty people were killed. The SS then went on the rampage and began burning synagogues. More than 250 were destroyed. In Jewish cemeteries, tombstone were knocked over or covered with anti-Semitic (that is, anti-Jewish) graffiti. Thousands of German Jews were arrested and sent to camps in Dachau, Sachsenhausen, or Büchenwald. The windows of 30,000 shops owned by Jews were smashed. The pieces of glass strewn over the streets gave the barbaric night the name *Kristallnacht*, or 'Night of Glass'.

The pretext for this outburst of violence was the assassination of a German diplomat in Paris by a young Polish Jew, Herschel Grynszpan. His intention was to avenge the victims of anti-Semitic persecutions organized by Hitler. As soon as he came to power, Hitler applied the measures he had spoken about in his book *Mein Kampf* (*My Struggle*), published in 1924. In this book he described his idea of a world based on a ranking of races. At the top was the 'Aryan' race. The German people were the best example of this race, whose destiny was to

Kristallnacht in a town on the River Rhine

A report drawn up on 14 November 1938 by the SS of the small town of Geldern on the River Rhine read as follows: 'We set fire to the synagogue of Geldern at approximately 4.00 a.m. At 9.00 a.m. it was entirely destroyed, including the surrounding walls. The interiors of two Jewish shops along with their small stock were totally destroyed.

After breaking the windows of houses belonging to other Jews, we completely demolished the furniture. Before 11.00 a.m. every Jewish man between fifteen and seventy had been arrested by the police. Throughout these activities the population remained passive. The fire in the synagogue attracted a rather large crowd of onlookers.'

The Volkswagen or 'people's car', which Hitler wanted every German family to have, was developed between 1934 and 1936. Actually, few of these vehicles were built before the war.

rule the world by eliminating or subduing 'inferior' races. On 7 April 1933, Hitler had a law passed which excluded Jews from government employment. He then prohibited them from working in liberal professions, or in jobs related to cultural activities (music, literature, films), before depriving them of their German nationality and the right to vote. Fleeing from repression and daily hardships, thousands of German Jews tried to move to democratic European countries or the United States. Some succeeded, but most did not. Many free countries closed their borders, even to those whose lives were in danger.

Hitler's theories were also based on the ideas of *Reich* (empire) and 'living space', which he continually referred to in his speeches. In his view, the German people's former unity had been destroyed by the 1919 Treaty of Versailles. This 'scrap of paper' had therefore to be destroyed by every means possible, and a Third Reich, or Third Empire created. (The First Empire lasted from AD 962 to 1806 under the name of the 'Holy Roman Empire'; The Second Empire lasted from 1871 to 1918 during the reigns of William I and William II.)

In order to accomplish this task, Hitler believed that Germany needed a *Führer* (leader), with absolute and unquestionable authority. After he came to power in 1933, with a solid 44 percent of the votes for his National Socialist (Nazi) Party, Hitler eliminated all opposition. Within a few months, he did away with all trade unions, and all political parties, except for his own.

In Nazi Germany, a constant watch was kept on every move made by each citizen. At

a very early age, men and women were recruited into mass organizations created for work and free time. Children and teenagers had to be members of Hitler's Youth Movement and become in the words of Hitler a 'brutal, bold, terrible . . . force which the world must fear'.

Newspapers, radio, and films were used to spread propaganda on the merits of the Nazi system. The German race and the history of Germany were distorted and glorified. The country's industrial, social, and military achievements were praised. Hitler's opponents were arrested, often beaten, and sent to concentration camps, which were first created in 1933. The political police (the Gestapo) and the black-uniformed security forces (the SS) maintained constant surveillance and stifled any sign of opposition. The swastika, which was black on a red background, was the Nazis' emblem and soon began to merit the description of it by the French writer François Mauriac, 'a black spider covered with blood'.

Hitler had a taste for spectacular mass-meetings which roused the crowds to a frenzy. The meeting places for these huge gatherings were decorated with many flags which he himself designed. On the flags was the swastika, a symbol of Aryan origin showing the course of the sun. According to Hitler, Aryans were the purest descendants of a people who were of Indo-European origin and had lived in ancient times. They were considered by the Nazis to be superior to all other human groups.

The Two Giants

On the eve of the Second World War, the United States and the USSR were the most powerful nations on the planet. With large populations, immense territories, and considerable natural resources, they stood as examples for the rest of the world. But both were faced with grave difficulties within their own borders.

After experiencing a period of tremendous prosperity in the 1920s, the United States was seriously affected by the economic crisis of 1929. Thousands of businesses and banks went bankrupt. Wheat, corn, and cotton prices collapsed. Thirteen million labourers and factory workers, farmers and office workers found themselves unemployed and without resources or relief.

In 1933, the newly elected president, Franklin D. Roosevelt, began a programme to put the nation back on its feet. In order to get the economy going again, he devalued the American dollar and gave the federal government a greater role in industrial and farm production. Little by little the country began to overcome the crisis, but in 1939 nine million people were still out of work. Nevertheless, America had regained hope and a certain amount of optimism for the future. The hundreds of films put out each year by Hollywood symbolized this new strength, which could also be seen in the success of the new comic book hero, Superman. This cartoon character was born in 1938. Practically invincible and as fast as the speed of light, he saved aeroplanes in distress, stopped high-speed trains and defeated his enemies. He became the symbol of a country regaining confidence in itself.

The USSR had chosen a different route from that of the United States. In November 1917, a revolution brought to power rulers who favoured Communism. Faced with enormous difficulties, and having to contend with the hostility of other nations after a two-

year civil war, the Soviet regime finally began to function under the leadership of Vladimir Lenin.

After Lenin died in 1924, Josef Stalin rose to power. A true dictator, out to crush any opposition, he began transforming the USSR into a modern, industrialized nation. Huge building sites appeared all over the country. The production of steel and electricity greatly increased. At the same time, Stalin decided to do away with the private ownership of farmland. He forced the peasants to work in farm co-operatives called kolkhozes. This collectivization by decree caused the death of at least three million peasants who refused to give up their land. With the same merciless violence, Stalin eliminated all those suspected of threatening his absolute power. Beginning in 1936, after a series of rigged trials, hundreds of thousands of civil servants, members of the Communist Party, and army officers were executed or sent to death camps in Siberia. This policy of terror was accompanied by widespread propaganda to encourage Soviet workers continually to produce more in factories and on farms. In August 1935, the miner Alexei Stakhanov was presented as a hero to be admired by other workers. According to the propaganda, he was reported to have dug 102 tonnes of coal in a day. That was fourteen times the amount normally extracted!

With Stakhanov and Superman, the USSR and the United States found themselves heroes who corresponded to their national pride. Nevertheless, the two giant countries, which in 1939 had few ideas in common, feared the same danger. They were worried about the war Germany seemed to be preparing and that Japan had already begun in China.

The success of the kolkhozes (farm co-operatives) was proclaimed on this red flag decorated with Stalin's portrait. The Soviet Union's agricultural prospects were, however, not very bright. The peasants, who represented more than 30 percent of the country's population, lived in harsh conditions. Victims of forced collectivization, they did not feel very motivated to increase yields or raise cattle. In an attempt to improve the country's food situation, Stalin had to grant them the right to own and cultivate a small plot of land and sell their produce on a free market.

The War in China

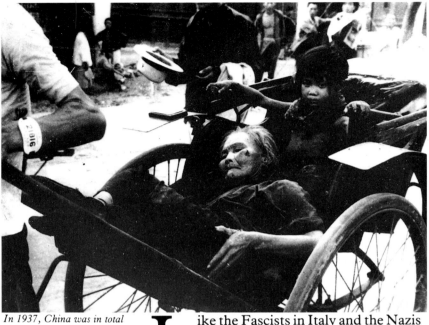

In 1937, China was in total chaos. Over 350 million peasants lived in misery. In addition to greedy landowners and heavy taxes, they also had to contend with natural disasters such as drought or flooding which devastated the countryside. China was no longer unified. Military leaders or warlords ruled entire provinces. Elsewhere in the 'red bases', Communists, who were led by Mao Tse-tung and continually pursued by government troops, were trying to establish a socialist society. In the large cities, foreign businessmen and military officers ruled over 'concessions'. These were neighbourhoods which were under their absolute control. Chiang Kai-shek, President of China since 1928, was having difficulties in imposing his authority over a country whose state of disorder constantly encouraged Japan's desire for expansion.

Like the Fascists in Italy and the Nazis in Germany, the Japanese army dreamed of great conquests. It wanted to create a *Dai Nippon*, or 'Greater Japan'. The military considered the Japanese islands and Korea (annexed by Japan in 1910) too small to sustain a population of sixty-five million inhabitants which increased each year by a million people. Furthermore, the Japanese economy, which had been hard hit by the crisis of 1929, was not self-sufficient. It needed iron, coal, oil, and cereals. All these were close by in the Chinese province of Manchuria, whose very name meant 'the land of plenty'.

In autumn 1931, claiming to be the victims of an act of sabotage (actually caused by themselves) of a railway they controlled, the Japanese entered Manchuria. They met little resistance from Chinese troops who retreated without fighting. For the first time since the First World War, a country had invaded another by force. When criticized by the League of Nations, the Japanese rejected the condemnation. In 1933 they left the League of Nations for good after extending their control southward over another Chinese province.

The governments of France, Great Britain, and the United States began to worry about Japan's ambitions, which threatened their interests in Asia. They were almost certain that the rest of China would be the next target for Japanese expansion. In 1936, the way was made easier for the imperialists. A group of extremists assassinated all the Japanese leaders who had remained pacifist and might have been able to oppose the military's ambitions.

On 7 July 1937, on the outskirts of Peking near the Marco Polo bridge, shooting broke out between Japanese and Chinese troops. The government in Tokyo now had the excuse it had waited for. It blamed the Chinese army for the incident and declared war on China.

The Japanese army, airforce, and navy launched an assault on a country weakened by civil war. China could offer little resistance. Its major cities fell one after another. Peking, Nanking, Canton, and Shanghai were all occupied. Some Chinese

Japanese Bombs in China

Behind the slope, as I climbed, was the red of spreading fire; and from the red bowl beyond the rim, people were fleeing. They were trudging on foot, fleeing in rickshaws, riding on sedan chairs, pushing wheelbarrows; and as they streamed out, an occasional limousine or army truck would honk or blast its way through the procession, which would part, then close, then continue its flight to the countryside. They carried mattresses, bedrolls, pots and pans, food, bits of furniture. They carried babies in their arms; grandmothers rode piggyback on men's shoulders; but they did not talk: in their silence one could even hear the padding shuffle of their feet.

At the crest, where one began the descent into the old city, I could get a broader view. The electric power lines had been bombed out; so, too, had the main pipe of Chungking's water system, which ran down the main street. There was no light but that of the fires, no water to fight the fires, which were spreading up and down the alleys of old Chungking. One could hear the bamboo joints popping as the fire ate timbers; now there was noise, women screamed, men yelled, babies cried. Some sat rocking back and forth on the ground, chanting. I could hear screaming in the back alleys; several times I saw people dart out into the main street, their clothes on fire, then roll over and over again to put out the flames.

Eyewitness account by American journalist Theodore H. White.

forces fought bravely but they did not have the modern weapons of their enemy. Japanese bombers and artillery wreaked havoc. The Japanese showed no mercy. Entire villages were slaughtered at the slightest sign of resistance. When Nanking was taken, Japanese soldiers killed their prisoners one by one, using some of them as dummies for bayonet training. Civilians were not spared. Roughly 200,000 of them were killed during the six-week massacre.

Now controlling China's vital regions, the Japanese planned to raise the flag of the Rising Sun over a growing empire. Strengthened by their victories, they dreamed of new battles and new conquests even if that meant facing the other great power of the Pacific, the United States. In order to carry out this aggressive policy, the Japanese signed an alliance with Hitler and Mussolini, making them even more a threat to world peace.

In this facsimile of one of the adventures of Tintin, The Blue Lotus, *the cartoonist, Hergé, relates almost exactly the incident of the Mukden railway which was used by the Japanese as a pretext to invade Manchuria.*

(Original French edition first published in 1936.)

A Swiss caricature published soon after the annexation of Austria by Germany (March 1938). Hitler is shown as a giant Gulliver surrounded by Lilliputians in the form of European politicians. The Pole, Joseph Beck, wearing a helmet, protects the Führer with a ridiculous umbrella. Hitler holds Mussolini, who is in his usual posture, on his left-hand finger. On Hitler's cap, members of the League of Nations sadly contemplate the Treaty of Versailles. In the left-hand corner, the French are playing leapfrog while to the right the peoples of Central Europe dance to the sound of the violin.

Threats to Peace

In 1933, Hitler began to work towards one of his major goals. This was to destroy the clauses of the Treaty of Versailles, even if it led to a world conflict.

The Treaty of Versailles limited the number of servicemen in the German army to 100,000 and prohibited the manufacture of modern military equipment (tanks, warplanes, and submarines). Through various deceptions, however, the Nazi leaders were able to equip the country with arms. Marshal Hermann Goering, who was responsible for civil aviation, created a 'League for Air Sports'. This seemingly peaceful organization was actually a cover for the training of future pilots for the *Luftwaffe*, the German airforce. Likewise, German companies prepared prototypes of fighter planes and tanks which could be mass-produced when the time came.

In 1935, mass production of this military equipment began, for Hitler had just decided to restore compulsory military service, in total defiance of one of the clauses of the Treaty of Versailles.

The war in Spain

The Spanish Civil War began in July 1936 with the rebellion of generals hostile to the Popular Front and its Republican government. It ended on 28 March 1939, with the victory of the rebels. Supported by the Church, rich landowners and the upper class, the rebels benefited from a powerful army and aid given by Hitler and Mussolini. The Republican government received arms and advisers sent by Stalin as well as help from 45,000 volunteers from the 'International Brigades' of fifty-three different countries. This merciless war, in which tens of thousands of civilians died, cost the lives of nearly 700,000 soldiers, and forced 350,000 individuals to flee the dictatorial regime of General Franco into exile.

France and Britain, who were responsible for enforcing the treaty, did nothing except express verbal indignation. Within a few months, the German arms industry was flourishing. Steelworks, metallurgical and chemical factories, aeroplane, tank and armoured vehicle manufacturers slowly began to supply Hitler with the means for his ambitions. In the spring of 1936, his propaganda minister, Goebbels, stated in a speech, 'It is more advantageous to import raw materials for arms than food . . . Let us tighten our belts, for it will do us some good. It will make us lighter and ready for action.' In addition to this industrial activity, the building of strategic roads, airfields, and railways enabled the Nazis to reduce unemployment and excite the nationalism of the German people.

In March 1936, Hitler once again violated the Treaty of Versailles. He sent troops into the Rhineland, a German province located between the left bank of the Rhine River and the borders of Holland, Belgium, and France. The demilitarization of the Rhineland had been demanded by the Allies (France, Britain, and Belgium) in 1919. Once again Britain and France did nothing.

In July of the same year, the Führer decided to help General Francisco Franco in Spain. Franco had just overthrown the lawfully elected republican government of the the Popular Front. Hitler sent him equipment, technicians, planes, and pilots. The Nazis saw the Spanish Civil War as a unique opportunity to train and experiment. They were able to test the effectiveness of their bombs. On 26 April 1937, German bombers attacked the small town of Guernica in Spain's Basque country. The terrifying raid left behind smoking ruins and 3,000 victims.

Another threat to peace was the alliance Hitler signed with the Italian dictator Mussolini. The two men shared the same taste for violence and the same hostility towards Communism. Both viewed war as the means of attaining their objectives, Yet, for a while Mussolini remained wary of Hitler. In 1935, however, the Führer was the only European head of state to support Mussolini during the Italian invasion of Ethiopia. Through this operation, Mussolini wanted to create an Italian colonial empire in East Africa. Italy had already controlled Libya and Somalia since the beginning of the twentieth century. In exchange for Hitler's support, Mussolini gave Hitler the go-ahead when the latter, with the help of Austrian Nazis, annexed Austria to Germany in March 1938. This annexation (or *Anschluss*) was another violation of the Treaty of Versailles. Hitler, however, could not have cared less.

On 8 May 1936, Mussolini received Hitler in Rome and wanted to impress him. In the ancient Roman Forum, he showed off his brand-new army. Thousands of people were there in Fascist uniforms, applauding the alliance between Mussolini and the Führer.

After the Munich Agreement had been signed, the London Daily Herald *came out with the headline, 'Mr. Chamberlain declares "It is peace for our time".' Chamberlain advised the crowd of Londoners welcoming him back 'to go home and sleep tight'.*

From Munich to Danzig

When it was created in 1919, Czechoslovakia was given a region inhabited mainly by Germans. This region was in the western part of the new country and was referred to as the Sudetenland. With prosperous industries and large mineral resources, it was essential to the Czech economy. Its mountainous terrain also gave the country an important natural line of defence. However, the integration into the Czech state of three million Germans in the Sudetenland proved difficult. A large majority of them were attached to their German heritage and rejected the authority of the government in Prague, capital of a Slav nation.

Hitler's rise to power encouraged Sudeten Germans to demand self-government and even integration into the Third Reich. They created a Nazi party which stepped up killings and violent demonstrations against the Czech authorities. In 1938, judging the time favourable, Hitler demanded the return of the Sudetenland to its German homeland. France and Britain, however, were responsible for Czechoslovakia's borders. While agreeing to take the Sudeten Germans' demands for self-government into account, the French and British refused to

Germans from the Sudetenland pull down the border post between Germany and Czechoslovakia which the Munich Agreement had just rendered useless. The German Reich recovered 30,000 square kilometres (11,500 square miles) and three million inhabitants.

be blackmailed by Hitler, who declared his readiness to go to war.

At the beginning of 1938, at a dinner party given by the French embassy in Berlin, Marshal Goering cynically joked, 'Look at the shape of Czechoslovakia. It goes against any common sense. It's Europe's appendix! It has to be operated on!'

As the months went by, the situation continued to worsen. In the summer of 1938, Hitler was ready to perform the 'operation' suggested by Goering. At the Nazi congress in Nuremberg on 12 September, the Führer demanded the immediate annexation of the Sudetenland. A few days later he even added that he would invade Czechoslovakia on the morning of 1 October if an agreement had not been reached by then.

All over Europe war was believed to be inevitable. Eager to preserve peace, however, France and Britain entered into negotiations. Mussolini volunteered to act as intermediary. On 28 September 1938, a last-chance conference was held in Munich while the German army was on its way to the Czech border. Meanwhile, France began to mobilize its army and Czecholovakia declared that it was prepared to withstand any invasion.

In fact, neither France nor Britain had any real intention of going to war over Czechoslovakia. The British Prime Minister, Neville Chamberlain, made this clear in a speech broadcast over the radio on the evening of 27 September. 'However great our sympathy for a small nation confronted with a large and powerful neighbour, we cannot under any circumstances whatsoever commit ourselves to leading the British Empire into a war solely for this small nation. If we have to fight, it must be for problems much vaster than this!'

From this Hitler understood that the French and British were ready to make any concession. During the Munich conference, the Führer obtained control of Sudeten territory which his troops entered on 1 October. Alone and abandoned by its allies, Czechoslovakia withdrew its regiments and gave up one of its richest provinces. A few months later, in defiance of the Munich Agreement, Hitler occupied most of the rest of the country. In March 1939, Nazi troops entered Prague. Czechoslovakia was removed from the map. France and Britain's

policy of appeasement had only whetted the appetite of the Third Reich.

Having seen the extent to which France and Britain seemed prepared to make concessions, Hitler now turned his attention towards Poland. He demanded the city of Danzig, and free passage in the corridor that linked the port of Danzig to the rest of Poland, but which divided Germany. This time France and Britain finally decided not to give way, but to help Poland. Hitler was not aware of the Allies' degree of determination, but to be on the safe side he started talks with the USSR. The Russians were unprepared for war, and the Germans were afraid of having to fight on two fronts simultaneously. Therefore, on 24 August 1939, to the general surprise of all, Hitler and Stalin signed a pact of non-aggression. From that point on Hitler was free to do as he wished in Poland, provided part of the country was given to the USSR as agreed in a secret clause of the pact.

On 1 September 1939, Hitler sent his armed forces into Poland. Hundreds of tanks moved on Warsaw and Poland's other major cities, which were also bombed by more than 2,000 planes. Keeping their promise, France and Britain declared war on Germany, and the Second World War began.

The Foreign Minister of the Soviet Union, Vyacheslav Molotov, and the German Foreign Secretary, Joachim von Ribbentrop, seal the signing of the German-Soviet pact in August 1939.

Blitzkreig and the 'Phoney War'

(extracts from the diary of Joseph Ménétrier)

Intended to protect the French border, the Maginot Line was named after the minister of war who built it. Completed in 1932, it formed a gigantic maze of large underground works including barracks, electric power stations, food and ammunition dumps that were all linked by tunnels to gun emplacements. The short-comings of this defensive system, however, were many. Its 75 mm guns had too short a range. It lacked an air-defence system, and above all it stopped at the Belgian border where the Germans, using the same successful strategy as in 1914, would invade France again.

The story of Joseph Ménétrier is typical. On 2 September 1939, he was conscripted like hundreds of thousands of other young Frenchmen. On 3 September France declared war on Germany in response to Hitler's invasion of Poland, but did not attack. Stationed on the eastern and northern fronts, the soldiers waited. This was the 'phoney war'.

Paris, 1 September 1939

I sat down at the Café Thénin to enjoy a cup of coffee as I do every morning. The first edition of today's newspaper gave, without comment, Hitler's demand for the 'Danzig Corridor'. He wanted to take this strip of territory which linked Poland to the Baltic Sea. A man came rushing in with the *Paris-Midi* newspaper in his hand shouting, 'They've invaded Poland!' Everyone in the café immediately surrounded him. In the midst of the overall commotion, it was announced that mobilization would begin tomorrow. We've had too many alerts over the past year for me to be surprised. Besides,

two days ago I saw the children from the school on rue de Marseilles leave for the countryside with their small satchels. They were being evacuated already. It was not a good sign. Despite my disgust of war, I think matters have gone too far. I'll go to war because it's necessary, but I won't go with a flower in my rifle like my father did at the beginning of the war in 1914.

I went home to put my affairs in order and prepare my haversack. I will slip this diary into it. In the evening I walked around Paris. Small groups had formed in front of posters announcing the general mobilization beginning on 2 September. A lot of people have already received instructions on where to go: I have to be in Nancy tomorrow.

Nancy, 3 September, in the evening

We had just been told that at eleven o'clock this morning, in reaction to Hitler's lightning attack on Poland, Britain and France declared war against Germany. I went on foot to the railway station to buy the *Petit Parisien* newspaper. At the restaurant in the station, people were discussing the latest news. The Germans had invaded Poland without declaring war. It was a total surprise. It was said that the Polish army did not even have time to mobilize all its soldiers! The Nazis used the method called 'lightning war', or *Blitzkreig* as they called it. Thousands of tanks overran the Polish

border backed up by swarms of planes from the *Luftwaffe*. According to the *Petit Parisien*, Polish defences had been instantly destroyed by a hail of bombs. The Polish airforce did not even have time to get its planes off the ground!

28 September 1939

Warsaw has fallen after heroic resistance. Not even a month was necessary for Hitler to remove the country from the map of Europe. But here everyone has been trying to reassure himself by repeating 'France isn't Poland'. Our army is powerful and we won't fight tanks with horses like the Poles. We're protected by the Maginot Line, which is supposed to stop any German invasion dead in its tracks. Whatever happens, we won't let ourselves be pushed around.

November 1939

I'm going to stop writing this diary because there's really nothing to tell at the moment. We're all getting bored and our morale is declining. Several of my comrades who left their families without support are wondering what they're doing here. This is a war of words and not of battles. Radio Stuttgart often broadcasts messages in French. A voice tells us that we fought enough in the First War, that this slaughter is useless and that the Führer only wants one thing and that is peace. The voice adds that

this absurd war will only be to the advantage of the British. German planes flying over our lines do not drop bombs but thousands of tracts repeating more or less the same thing as on the radio. Even if we know it's propaganda and refuse to believe what the Germans tell us, it's demoralizing. We spend our days playing cards, and reading newspapers. We also drink a lot. I don't know who invented the expression a 'phoney war' to describe the predicament of idle soldiers but it's a good one.

The 'Stuka' was the name of a fighter bomber which was the key weapon of the Blitzkreig. Faster than a conventional bomber, it could carry a tonne of bombs, and its dive attacks were terrifyingly effective. A wave of 'Stukas' could in one attack put an airfield out of operation, destroy a bridge and stop a column of soldiers dead in their tracks. The siren that the pilot turned on during the dive heightened the effect of terror on the soldiers or civilians being attacked.

The French felt that they lived in a country where people smiled and ate and drank to their hearts' content, whereas Germany was considered a country of ersatz (substitute) products, such as margarine instead of butter. It was a country where people could not be anything but weak and fragile!

The Fall of France

The weather was beautiful at the beginning of May 1940. As on every day over the past eighteen months, British and French soldiers stationed on the front waited in a state of boredom. In April the Germans had invaded Denmark and Norway, but now the phoney war seemed to have returned. In Germany, on the other side of the River Rhine, however, armoured divisions were assembling and dozens of warplanes were preparing to take off. The German army staff was waiting for the return of good weather before advancing further into Western Europe.

On 10 May at 4.30 a.m. French soldiers were woken by successive waves of low-flying planes. The German war machine was on the move. Surprised, but confident in their defences, the French generals and government announced that everything was ready to confront Hitler's army.

Within a few days, German troops occupied the Netherlands, Belgium and Luxembourg. As in 1914, the Germans prepared to invade France by way of the great northern plains. They used the same strategy which had proved so successful in Poland, the *Blitzkreig*. The German planes, Stukas, were designed for dive-bombing, spreading terror and death among their foes. They were followed by armoured divisions which each attacked precise points on the front, breaking up the lines of defence.

Three days after the general offensive had begun, the Germans broke through the French lines of defence at Sedan. Demoralized, and poorly prepared for this new type of war, French and British troops retreated to the French coast and converged on Dunkirk. At the end of May, 350,000 men were trapped there by the advancing Germans. A fleet of boats of all kinds approached the beaches where the troops had gathered, and attempted to embark the soldiers to take them to Britain. They saved 200,000 men in this way. But thousands of others were cut down by bullets and bombs from the German planes. They died on beaches already littered with abandoned military equipment. Those left behind by the boats joined the tens of thousands of prisoners already taken.

The German army moved south. It crossed the River Somme, then the Seine near the city of Rouen, which had been

heavily bombed. On 10 June, Italy declared war against France, but French mountain infantrymen repelled the assault by Italian troops in the Alps and around Menton.

Everywhere the French army seemed to be falling apart. Huge columns of people filled the roads, driven on by the German advance. Fleeing soldiers and officers mixed with the hundreds of thousands of civilians. On foot, by car, cart, or bicycle, everyone fled the battle zone. Sometimes German or Italian planes attacked the long lines of traffic and refugees. When this happened everyone left their vehicles and belongings and jumped into ditches to protect themselves from the hail of bullets sweeping the road.

Faced with the unstoppable German advance, which was delayed only by a few brave units, the President of the Council of Ministers, Paul Reynaud, decided to leave Paris for Bordeaux. The capital was declared an 'open city'. In Bordeaux, ministers and deputies were divided. Some wanted to continue fighting alongside Britain at all costs. Others wanted the hostilities to cease. The President of the Republic, Albert Lebrun, favoured the latter view and decided to replace Paul Reynaud with the old and famous Marshal Henri Philippe Pétain.

On 17 June, all those with radios heard the quavering voice of this old man say, 'It is with a broken heart that I ask you today to stop fighting.'

The armistice was signed a week later in the town of Rethondes, near Compiègne, in the same railway car in which the Germans had signed the ceasefire in 1918. Most of the country accepted the armistice with relief. People still on the road, sleeping outside and scavenging for food, had only one thing in mind, and that was that they would be able to go home. Few Frenchmen realized that their country was going to have to pay dearly for their surrender.

Nevertheless, a handful of people decided not to give in and continued the fight. Among them was General Charles de Gaulle, former Secretary of War, who left Bordeaux for London on 17 June. On the 18th, he appealed to his fellow countrymen on the BBC: 'Whatever happens, the flame of French resistance must not go out and will not go out.' Few people were listening, and not many wanted to join him. However, he embodied the honour of France.

On the morning of 24 June 1940, Hitler arrived in Paris unannounced. Like any good tourist, he viewed the capital from the heights of Montmartre, admired the opera house, the Madeleine, the Arc de Triomphe, the Invalides and Napoleon's tomb. 'It was the dream of my life', he confided to one of his close advisers.

"LET US
GO FORWARD
TOGETHER"

Britain Stands Alone

On 19 July 1940, victory celebrations were organized throughout Germany. After only a few months of war, the Nazi flag flew over France, Belgium, Holland, Denmark, and Norway. Most other European countries either were Hitler's allies (like Italy) or took a neutral stand (like the USSR, Spain, and Sweden). But on the other side of the English Channel, an opponent refused to lay down its arms. Behind their prime minister, Winston Churchill, who promised them only 'blood, toil, tears, and sweat', the British united. The entire country was determined to fight and repel a possible landing of German troops. Miles of trenches and dozens of shelters were dug out along the English coast. Ports were fortified.

Hitler, meanwhile, had an invasion plan prepared. He attempted to put together an armada of ships, soldiers, and planes to invade England. But first he had to control the skies and break the morale of the British. To do that, he was counting on the *Luftwaffe*. Between July and October 1940, the Battle of Britain took place. The towns in the southern part of the country were regularly bombed. At times London was literally in flames. For fifty-seven consecutive nights an average of 200 bombers dropped explosive, incendiary, and time bombs. Yet, despite this relentless pounding, the British population's morale remained unshakeable, and the military counterattack was effective. The fighter planes from the Royal Air Force and anti-aircraft guns decimated the German airforce. By 31 October 1940, the *Luftwaffe* had lost 1,750 of the 2,700 planes used in battle since the month of July. A German landing was now out of the question. Furious with the change in plans, Marshal Goering decided to destroy the industrial city of Coventry. On the night of 14 November, 500 bombers dropped 600 tonnes of explosives on it. The verb 'to coventry' came to mean the total destruction of a city.

Britain had survived, thanks to a few hundred pilots. They were mostly British, of course, but there were also those who had survived the battles on the Continent. They came from Norway, Holland, Belgium, Poland, and France, and all had refused to give in.

Many others also contributed to this British victory. For example, scientists and electronics engineers developed a new means of defence called 'radar' (Radio Detection and Ranging). This invention picked up the German planes as soon as they arrived over the Channel or the North Sea, and indicated their positions to the British fighter planes.

With the collapse of Western Europe in the face of the Nazi assault, London became more than ever before the last hope of resistance to Hitler. Several of the governments which fled the German conquest found refuge in the British capital. They provided Winston Churchill with reinforcements of thousands of volunteers, with the support of ships which had escaped the Germans, and above all with the resources of their colonies.

Confronted by Hitler, Britain could also rely on its dominions (such as Australia, Canada, and New Zealand), colonies (including India, Kenya, and Nigeria), and protectorates (Egypt, for example). It could also count on the support of the United States, which had remained neutral since the beginning of the war but which was helping Britain by providing arms and raw materials.

From 30 September 1940 to 10 May 1941, London and its surrounding areas were subjected to the Blitz. Every night fires lit up the sky, and German planes droned back and forth while the searchlights of anti-aircraft guns tried to find them. After months of blind destruction, several tens of thousands of buildings and homes had been demolished or damaged. Over 40,000 dead bodies and as many wounded were pulled out of the ruins. And yet, the morale of Londoners, like that of all the British, was amazing. They identified themselves with Churchill (opposite) the 'old lion' who embodied the will to continue the war, refused all offers of an armistice, and foresaw only one solution, final victory. Each night the inhabitants of London went down into the safety of the underground.

Vichy France

Right: Marshal Pétain is shown in the folds of the French flag, wearing the medal of the Legion of Honour. The France represented in this poster is that of the peasants and craftsmen who were considered guardians of the eternal values of work, family and homeland. This is the France the Marshal liked to meet with during his numerous trips (below).

After their victory over France, the Germans decided to divide the country into several zones. In the east they simply annexed Alsace and a part of Lorraine, which became one of the provinces of the Third Reich. German troops occupied the area north of the River Loire and along the coast of the English Channel and the Atlantic Ocean. French administration was left intact. Finally, in the south they created what was called a 'free' zone. Here a government headed by Marshal Pétain, with whom the Germans hoped to have good relations, was in power. Between the 'occupied' northern zone and the 'free' southern zone ran a 'demarcation line', a border controlled by the Germans.

On 10 July 1940, a few weeks after the collapse of the French army, a majority of French deputies and senators meeting in Vichy handed power over to Henri Philippe Pétain. Victor of the Battle of Verdun in the First World War, and Marshal of France, this haughty old man put an end to the French Third Republic and took the title of Head of the French State. He replaced the republican motto 'Liberty, Equality, Fraternity' by 'Work, Family, Homeland'. He wanted to give the French people, among whom he enjoyed immense popularity, the image of a ruler and father who sacrificed himself for the common good. His colleagues, mainly right-wing politicians, encouraged him to set up an authoritarian, racist, and nationalistic regime.

Relying on anti-Jewish feelings among the population, the government of Marshal Pétain and his prime minister Pierre Laval passed a 'Law on Jews'. Frenchmen who practised the Jewish religion were no longer allowed to work in a profession related to teaching, the law, or the army. Freemasons and militant communists were victims of similar restrictions. Foreign Jews were penned up in camps. The Press was censored, schools were kept under a close watch, and trade unions were outlawed.

A strong personality cult developed around Marshal Pétain. His picture was everywhere, in homes, schools, and public

buildings. His face was on stamps, postcards, school exercise books, and buttons. Songs and hymns were composed in praise of him. Books, newspapers, comic strips, and films were devoted to his life, ideas, and actions. Many French truly believed that Pétain was a defence against Hitler's demands, and that the old man had saved them from still greater disasters.

On 24 October 1940, in the small town of Montoire, in the heart of France, Pétain met Hitler. On the advice of Pierre Laval, the old Marshal had agreed to have talks with the Chancellor of the Reich. Before photographers, the two men shook hands. Had the Marshal not stated a few days before that he was ready to 'collaborate in all areas'? Little by little, despite a few feeble signs of refusal, Pétain and his government were to be lured into ever-closer collaboration with the Germans. Whether willingly or through force, the Vichy government of Pétain became a satellite of Nazi Germany, especially after November 1942 when the German army crossed the demarcation line and took control of the 'free' zone and thus the entire country. By this time, the British and Americans had landed in the French colonies of Morocco and Algeria in northern Africa, and the Germans feared the south of France would be their next objective.

Many people advised Pétain to join the British and Americans (the Allies) in North Africa. However, he decided to remain in Vichy where his policy of collaboration led him to total submission to the Germans. He supported the creation of the anti-Communist LVF (Legion of French

Volunteers) made up of young French soldiers fighting for the Germans in the USSR. Pétain also encouraged workers to go to Germany to help with the war effort, and he supported the Germans in their struggle against people who resisted their rule.

Montoire, 20 July 1940. A handshake between Hitler and Pétain committed France to collaboration with the Germans.

In order to get through the 'demarcation line', people had to have a pass, issued by the Germans in very limited numbers. Many people could not get one, for example Jews, Resistance fighters, army deserters, and British pilots who had parachuted from their planes when they were shot down. They had to rely on the people who took them secretly across the demarcation line.

German-Occupied Paris

Declared an 'open city', Paris did not fight. Not one single monument or building was destroyed. Paris still looked like Paris, yet everything had changed. The Germans were in occupation. On 15 June 1940, they entered a Paris deserted by most of its inhabitants. Flags with the swastika flew everywhere. At the Place de la Concorde, signs in German indicated the direction of Lille, Metz, or Le Havre to trucks carrying troops. At crossroads, German policemen directed the flow of military convoys. The steel mesh collar on their uniforms prompted Parisians to name them ironically 'dog collars' or 'first class cows'.

Flats, hospitals, cinemas, and restaurants were taken over. The German army set up headquarters in luxurious buildings on the Champs-Elysées, the major boulevards, rue Royale, and avenue Kléber. The Empire theatre became the 'theatre for German soldiers' and the Rex cinema was set aside exclusively for them.

The German secret police, the Gestapo, moved into buildings on rue des Saussaies and avenue Foch. These addresses came to mean death for those taken there. Men and women suspected of being Resistance fighters were mercilessly tortured.

Despite the imposition of a curfew, life in Paris under Nazi rule remained surprisingly lively. People returned to the city, and theatres, cabarets, and music halls filled up again. The racetrack in Auteuil reopened in autumn 1940. At the German embassy in Paris, German ambassador Otto Abetz threw lavish parties for the élite of Paris, the writers, actors, journalists, and artists. Without collaborating with the enemy, they accepted its presence. The poet, Jean Cocteau, attended the preview of the Third Reich's official sculptor, Arno Breker. Maurice Chevalier, Edith Piaf, Charles Trenet, and Tino Rossi continued to make records and give gala performances. Film stars did not all refuse to work in the film studios in Berlin.

Newspapers reappeared on the stands but they were censored by the Germans, who supplied the ink, paper, and money, without which they would not have been able to be published. The newspapers became the mouthpieces of the Germans. Journalists described Germany as invincible and Communism as evil. They denounced the

British, Jews, and Resistance fighters, whom they accused of continuing the war.

Radio Paris broadcast the same ideas, but Parisians wanting to escape this 'brainwashing' began, like many other French people, to listen secretly to Radio London. This station broadcast programmes in French presented by those who had joined de Gaulle in his refusal to accept defeat.

In these broadcasts, in which the 'French spoke to the French', humour alternated with serious topics. Pierre Dac was often heard humming the famous tune of the 'Cucaracha', 'Radio-Paris lies, Radio-Paris lies, Radio-Paris is German'. Resistance fighters also listened for coded messages intended for them, right up to the evening of 5 June 1944 when the lines of a poem by Verlaine announced that the time had come for the Allied landings.

Other Frenchmen chose to collaborate with the Nazis, for example, Jacques Doriot, founder before the war of the French People's Party, the writer Robert Brasillach, and the journalist Philippe Henriot. Others hunted down Jews or reported Resistance fighters, collaborated for personal profit, did business with the enemy, or agreed to put their factories or enterprises at the service of the German war effort. However, most of the people in Paris put up with the German occupation without either helping it or

opposing it with violence. For two million people, it was a matter of adapting to the way things were. Their real concern was finding enough food to eat and enough fuel to heat their homes during the long, harsh winters of the occupation.

The Institute for the Study of Jewish issues, on official service created by the Vichy government in 1941, was responsible for informing Frenchmen of the 'Jewish danger'. In its pamphlets, it repeated the racist theories common to all European countries occupied by the Nazis. On 5 September 1941, at the Berlitz Palace, and on the major boulevards, the exhibition 'The Jews and France' was opened. The newspapers and radio gave it enormous publicity. Tens of thousands of French people visited it.

The Opera square in Paris is covered with signs to direct German soldiers.

Operation Barbarossa

On 22 June 1941, at 4.00 a.m., Stalin was asleep in his country house near Moscow. Suddenly the telephone rang. 'We've been invaded', announced the voice of General Zhukov, Chief of the General Staff of the Soviet army.

Stalin was dumbfounded. He always believed that the pact signed with Germany in August 1939 would never be broken. Had he not at the time declared that 'the friendship between the peoples of Germany and the Soviet Union, joined together by blood, has every reason to last'? Information from several sources had warned Stalin of a possible attack by the Germans in the spring of 1941. But he was taken totally by surprise when operation 'Barbarossa', prepared by Hitler in December 1940, was put into action. The name Barbarossa referred to the twelfth-century Germanic emperor, Frederick I, or Frederick Barbarossa (Redbeard), This code name stood for a surprise attack whose aim was to reach the River Volga and the region of the Caucasus before the onset of winter.

Like Stalin, the Soviet Union's generals and troops, spread along the border, were surprised by the swiftness and power of the German army. The Germans were supported by Hitler's allies the Finns in the north and the Romanians in the south. The three million men, 10,000 tanks and 3,000 planes sent into action by the Germans crushed the first lines of Soviet defence, wiped out entire regiments, and destroyed planes and airports within just two weeks. On 10 July the Germans and their allies advanced between 400 and 800 kilometres (250–500 miles), depending on the area. The Baltic provinces, Belorussia, and a large part of the Ukraine fell to the invaders. The Soviets lost hundreds of tanks; tens of thousands of men died and over 300,000 were taken prisoner. But Russian resistance was often heroic and the T 34 tank created havoc among the German armoured divisions. A German

In the Crimea families come to identify their relatives massacred by the Germans. For Hitler, the war in the east was not a war like the others. He gave the order to his troops to exterminate Jews and members of the Communist Party in towns and villages. In 1941, Himmler, head of the SS, criticized German senior military officers for showing too much 'compassion' towards the civilian population. As in Poland, the war in Russia was one of extermination.

general even said that the Russians 'set fire to his armoured tanks like boxes of matches'.

At first, Stalin was taken aback, but he soon pulled himself together. In a speech, he outlined the main point of the strategy to be followed by the entire country. Each time the Red Army had to retreat, machines, means of transport, cereals, cattle and oil were all to be evacuated, or else destroyed. In the occupied territories, uncaptured soldiers and partisan units would have to resort to guerrilla warfare against the enemy.

This speech, accompanied by effective reorganization measures for the army, strengthened Soviet willpower. On the road to Moscow, the Germans came up against such fierce resistance that, at the end of July, Hitler abandoned his plans to advance on the capital. He ordered instead that some troops should turn south and conquer the oilfields of the Caucasus and the coal mines of the Donetz Basin, and that others should head north to capture Leningrad. On 30 August 1941, the city was surrounded by the Germans, and a 900-day siege began. Soldiers and civilians transformed Leningrad into a fortress. More than 550 kilometres (350 miles) of trenches, 30 kilometres (20 miles) of barricades, and 15,000 blockhouses were built. Hitler relied on a ruthless blockade to starve the population into submission.

In many places, despite the disorganization and lack of preparation of the Soviet army, German troops came up against pockets of resistance, where isolated units fought to the death to delay the German advance. The capture of numerous villages, of even simple log cabins, sometimes meant fierce struggles.

While the Germans were rejoicing over their victory and posing with a flag captured from the enemy, the first Russian prisoners were on their way to concentration camps. After eighteen days of fighting, there were 300,000 of them, and their fate turned out to be atrocious. The USSR had not signed the Geneva Convention which protected prisoners of war. Hitler took advantage of this and imposed a regime of forced labour on the Russian prisoners, which they had to accomplish on what amounted to starvation rations. Isolated from prisoners of other nations, the death rate in the Soviet camps was appalling.

During the winter months of 1941–42, the inhabitants of Leningrad lived in appalling conditions. People ate crows, cats, and dogs. They burned books and furniture to obtain a little warmth. Exhausted and starving, they suffered and died in the streets. As no one had the strength any longer to dig graves in the frozen ground of the cemeteries, huge communal graves were made with dynamite. In 900 days of siege, over 500,000 people died of famine and cold.

At the Gates of Moscow

During the first few days of October 1941, one and a half million men, 1,800 tanks, and 1,500 planes set out to capture Moscow. For Hitler's troops, it was a race against time. They had to advance almost 300 kilometres (200 miles) and take the city before the terrible Russian winter arrived.

Favoured at first by splendid weather, the German offensive crushed the first Soviet line of defence. Within a few days all roads leading to the capital were open. As in the Ukraine, tens of thousands of prisoners were taken. Panic overtook Moscow. Men, women, and children took to the road, fleeing before the enemy. On 18 October diplomats, leaders of the Communist Party, and members of the governments also left the city, which was mined with explosives ready to go off if the Germans entered.

Soon, however, the German army had to slacken its pace. It was confronted with the Russian autumn when snowstorms alternated with torrential rains which soaked the ground. This was the world of mud which Napoleon had described in 1812 as the 'fifth element'. Armoured vehicles, motorcycles, and tanks became stuck on roads unfit for travel. At times the ground froze, turning into one big skating rink. German soldiers began to suffer from the cold. The German command was paralysed by anxiety, haunted by visions of Napoleon's great army, which was defeated in 1812 by 'General Winter'.

Zhukov used the Germans' problems to his advantage. He had reinforcements sent from the Far East and he mobilized the people of Moscow to build trenches, shelters, and anti-tank ditches. On 13 October he addressed his troops, 'At present, everyone from the lowly soldier of the Red Army all the way up to its most senior officer has to fight

bravely and without hesitation for his homeland. And in Moscow . . . the fearful sowers of panic who abandon the field of battle, leave their posts without permission, or throw down their arms or tools, will be immediately shot'.

On 7 November, the anniversary of the Russian Communist revolution in 1917, Stalin presided over a large military parade in Moscow's Red Square. The Germans were only 50 kilometres (30 miles) away. In the threatened city, protected from the *Luftwaffe's* raids by anti-aircraft guns he gave a short speech: 'The eyes of the entire world are fixed on you, on the only force capable of exterminating that gang of hoodlums, the German intruders. The people of Europe are looking to you, for they have fallen into slavery under the yoke of the German conquerors. They are looking to you, their future liberators!'

Meanwhile, the German command decided to make a last assault on Moscow before the onset of January's sub-zero temperatures. Time was precious, and the troops lacked warm clothes, fuel, and food. On 2 December the German army came within 25 kilometres (15 miles) of Moscow. It was to go no further. Four days later, the Red Army launched its counteroffensive. Well armed, well equipped, and well commanded, the Soviet regiments pushed back the German troops who were exhausted after six months of continuous fighting. Everywhere the Germans retreated, abandoning along their way tanks and vehicles which the cold or lack of fuel prevented from working. By the end of the month, the noose around Moscow had loosened. For the first time since September 1939, the German army had suffered defeat. The Russian campaign that Hitler wanted to be glorious and rapid, stopped at the gates of Moscow. Of the three million men engaged in fighting on 22 June 1941, the Germans had already lost over 800,000 killed, wounded, or taken prisoner – more than one soldier in every four.

In October 1941, while the Germans were just outside the Soviet capital, Stalin attended the traditional military review, which each year celebrated the Russian revolution. The troops parading before government officials immediately left for the front where the Germans had broken through on 6 October.

31

Pearl Harbor

On Sunday 7 December 1941, in the Hawaiian Islands where the major part of the United States Pacific fleet was concentrated, most of the staff of the American base of Pearl Harbor had left for the weekend. Since the end of November, however, a Japanese fleet commanded by Admiral Isoroku Yamamoto had been secretly making its way toward the islands without arousing suspicion.

At 6.00 a.m., 183 Japanese torpedo, bomber, and dive-bomber planes, backed up by fighters, left the fleet and headed directly for the island of Oahu. On the American ships it was time to change guard. At approximately 7.50 a.m., the guards on board the battleships were getting ready for the ceremony of saluting the flag when they saw enemy planes diving in attack formation to unleash their lethal cagoes of bombs. The suddenness of the attack gave the Americans no time to respond. Fifteen minutes later, a second wave of 170 planes came and finished the attack. By 9.45 a.m., it was all over. American losses were considerable. Two battleships had been put out of action, 6 had been damaged, and 159 planes had been totally destroyed. There were 2,334 dead and 1,341 wounded. But the three aircraft carriers which were the aggressor's main target remained intact. Crusing at sea, they had been able to escape the destruction.

For the United States, 7 December 1941, became, in the words of President Roosevelt, 'an eternal day of infamy'. The American people reacted angrily to the Japanese aggression. All the necessary funds for a war which looked as though it would be long were unanimously voted by members of Congress. Four days after the raid on Pearl Harbor, Japan's faithful allies, the Germans and Italians, declared war on the United States, which was sure of Britain's support. The conflict was now truly on a world scale. Not one single inhabited continent or ocean on the globe was to be spared from the fighting.

In the Pacific, the Japanese began attacking British, Dutch, and American possessions. One by one, the British were forced to give up Hong Kong, Malaysia, Singapore, and Burma. The Dutch were not able to hold out in Indonesia, which came under Japanese control in March 1942, and the Americans were overwhelmed in the Philippine Islands, which were occupied by the Japanese at the beginning of May. The American general, Douglas MacArthur, who was defending the Philippines, left for Australia by submarine after promising, 'I shall return'.

Everywhere, Japan seemed to have been victorious. Her imperialistic ambitions included not only Manchuria and the main regions of China, but Indo-China (where Vichy France had accepted the presence of Japanese troops in 1940), Southeast Asia, and the large archipelagos of Indonesia and the Philippines. But the Japanese generals who led their country into the conquest of this empire underestimated the power of the United States and the Americans' fierce desire for revenge after Pearl Harbor.

On 18 April 1942, twenty-four American light bombers bombed Tokyo, to the total astonishment of the Japanese. On 9 May, after a long battle, the Japanese were prevented from taking total control of New Guinea. This air and sea confrontation in the Coral Sea put an end to the Japanese advance in the Pacific and paved the way for the first major Japanese defeat on Midway.

The Americans had not foreseen the possibility of a Japanese attack against Pearl Harbour. They feared a surprise offensive but thought that it would take place near the Philippines or in Indonesia. Several disturbing signs (radar signals, minisubmarines detected near the islands of Hawaii) had not been taken seriously. Luckily, not a single American aircraft carrier was in the harbour at the time of the attack. After the disaster, posters all over the United States announced that the victims of Pearl Harbour had not died in vain and that they would be avenged. The poster below uses words from Abraham Lincoln's 1863 Gettysburg address to make its point.

...we here highly resolve that these dead shall not have died in vain...

REMEMBER DEC. 7th!

A small boat rescues a sailor from the USS West Virginia, sunk by Japanese torpedoes and bombs.

The Pacific on Fire

On the morning of 5 May 1942, an impressive armada left Japan's ports. Admiral Yamamoto was in charge and had under his command 6,000 soldiers and sailors, 40 large warships, 8 aircraft carriers with 500 planes, and 200 additional ships. The huge fleet headed due east towards the tiny American atoll in the middle of the Pacific, almost 1,500 kilometres (900 miles) from the Japanese coast. The atoll was named Midway because of its central position between Asia and North America.

For the Japanese, the possession of these few pieces of land barely above sea level was an essential strategic objective. To get a

Bordering India and China, the country of Burma had a major strategic position throughout the Second World War. The Japanese fought Anglo-American forces there for a long time in order to obtain control of the roads and bridges built by the Americans to supply their Chinese allies.

foothold on Midway meant obtaining effective protection against any surprise attack likely to come from the east. It also meant being able to threaten the west coast of the USA.

Yamamoto saw another advantage in the operation. He hoped that a large part of the American fleet would come to the rescue of the threatened atoll. With overwhelming naval superiority, he expected to finish the task begun six months earlier at Pearl Harbor. If everything went as planned, the United States would suffer a defeat so severe that it would not have any choice but to negotiate for peace.

In order for his plan to work, Yamamoto was counting on surprise. He did not know, however, that American intelligence services were aware of his secret offensive. A few weeks before, the code-breakers of the United States Navy had managed to crack the communication code used by the Japanese navy. The American Admiral, Chester Nimitz, could read his enemy's plan! Notified of the planned attack on Midway, he reinforced the atoll's defences and brought in three aircraft carriers to oppose the enemy's squadrons.

Nearly a month after leaving Japan, part of the Japanese fleet was within close range of Midway in the early hours of 3 June. An air attack began to prepare for the landing of Japanese troops. There was extensive damage, and the American planes based on the island were unable to inflict much damage on the attackers. Everything seemed to be going according to Yamamoto's plans, but halfway through the morning of 4 June, fate suddenly favoured Admiral Nimitz.

Waves of American dive bombers appeared out of the sky, having taken off from aircraft carriers that the Japanese had failed to locate correctly. As they swooped down on the Japanese air and sea fleet, they had an extraordinary stroke of luck. They discovered beneath them decks loaded with Japanese planes preparing to take off. Each American bomb exploding in the middle of these aircraft caused considerable damage. Soon, three Japanese aircraft carriers were in flames. Their firefighting squads were not able to put out the fires which spread from the decks to the holds, from the planes to the ammunition stores. A few hours later, a fourth aircraft carrier was also sent to the bottom of the ocean.

Faced with defeat, Yamamoto was afraid to send his large battleships against Midway without air protection, so he gave the order to retreat. Slowly, the Japanese ships turned back towards Japan. In order to escape the American planes which were now masters of the sky, they let off artificial smoke and tried to take advantage of the bad weather.

For Japan, Midway was a total defeat. None of the objectives set by Yamamoto had been realized. His navy had lost a dozen ships including a heavy cruiser and four aircraft carriers. Two hundred and fifty planes had been shot down, and 3,500 men had been killed, among then a hundred of the best airmen. The Americans lost only one aircraft carrier, and the Stars and Stripes still flew over Midway. On the evening of 'glorious 4 June', celebrated all over America, Admiral Nimitz felt as if he had partly avenged the dead of Pearl Harbor. The Japanese fleet no longer ruled the Pacific Ocean.

The battle of Midway also showed what a decisive role was to be played in the future by the co-ordination of air and sea forces. The aircraft carrier was to be the key to all victories in the Pacific.

During the Pacific war, aircraft carriers were protected by a fleet of destroyers. They were also equipped with powerful radar systems and deadly anti-aircraft guns capable of destroying most enemy attacks. On board, safety teams stood by, ready to put out fires and repair damage caused by enemy planes which had escaped the ship's gunfire.

The Battle of the Atlantic

A German U-boat emerges from the ocean, its mission of destruction accomplished. In 1942, 400 German submarines were in operation. The most modern were equipped with gas turbines and reached a speed of 23 knots (40 kilometres per hour) below the surface. Their T5 torpedoes were guided by the sound of the boat they were fired at and rarely missed their target.

On 3 September 1939, the same day as war was declared, the torpedoing by a German submarine of the British ocean liner, the *Athenian*, marked the beginning of a battle which would not end until 8 May 1945. It was a battle on several fronts spread over the Atlantic Ocean.

In the summer of 1940, the Germans had still not been able to conquer Britain and decided to blockade the British Isles. From ports in occupied France — Brest, Lorient, Saint-Nazaire, La Pallice — their U-boats (submarines) launched attacks designed to destroy all shipping using British ports. For Admiral Karl Doenitz who commanded them, the U-boats were the 'backbone of the fight against Britain'. He achieved spectacular results. The tonnage of British ships sunk far exceeded that of ships being built and put into service. The British tried to defend themselves with submarine detection techniques (Asdic and Sonar), convoys, and depth charges but their losses remained high.

At the end of 1941 and in 1942, following the entry of the United States into the conflict, the submarine war spread across the entire Atlantic. From Greenland to the Gulf of Mexico, from the coast of Africa all the way to South America, German U-boats lay in wait. Hitler and Doenitz wanted at all costs to prevent American war materials from reaching the battle fronts. Sinking an average-sized cargo vessel meant sending 20 armoured cars, as many lorries, 30 automatic machine guns, and 1,000 tonnes of ammunition and supplies to the bottom.

In five months the United States lost 505 ships, of which 112 were oil tankers, off the coast of Central America. In view of their unexpected success, the Germans decided to step up their U-boat building programme. They increased the number built from 60 in September 1939 to 250 in the spring of 1942. They made technical improvements that extended the submarines' range. The Germans' tactics were based on the idea of 'wolf packs'. The submarines operated in groups and often at night. After locating their target, they surfaced and fired their torpedoes on the convoys before resubmerging to reload their torpedo tubes. Usually the attacks continued all night.

The U-boats also threatened convoys headed for the USSR. These were easy targets for the German ships hiding in the fjords of Norway. The sea route linking America with the Soviet port of Murmansk became the most deadly of the war. It was so dangerous that the Americans had to abandon it in July 1942. Likewise, Allied convoys sailing to Egypt or the Middle East rarely took the Mediterranean route where they were very vulnerable. They went around Africa (where they still suffered attacks by German U-boats and Italian submarines off the coast of Dakar) and arrived in Egypt by way of the Indian Ocean

and the Red Sea.

Confronted with this worrying situation, which risked ruining entirely their military efforts, the British and Americans improved the protection of their ships. Convoys no longer sailed unless tightly surrounded by fast, anti-submarine warships such as destroyers or corvettes, and small aircraft carriers whose planes kept watch over the waters. Meanwhile, improved detection methods and more powerful anti-submarine depth charges enabled the Allies to reverse the situation. In 1943, and especially in1944, German U-boats suffered heavy losses and more ended up at the bottom of the ocean than were being built in Baltic ports. The Allies finally won the battle of the Atlantic. At the end of the war, they had sunk 781 German U-boats and 85 Italian submarines.

By November 1943, the Germans had already built gigantic block-houses in ports, and they decided to construct concrete walls along the coast of the North Sea, the English Channel and the Atlantic. The 'Atlantic Wall' mobilized thousands of workers. Over 10,000 block-houses were built. They hid guns with 28 different calibres, such as the 406 mm one in the picture. This was one of the largest guns ever used during the war.

The War in the Mediterranean

A bomber of the Luftwaffe *flies over the Acropolis in Athens. On 27 April 1941, the Nazi flag was flying over the Parthenon.*

On 27 November 1942 at 6.00 a.m., the French fleet was scuttled in Toulon harbour. France lost half of its capital ships. Only five submarines managed to leave the harbour and join the Allied forces in North Africa.

Rommel, the 'desert fox'

For four years, the Mediterranean and the surrounding area was the centre of constant and deadly battles on land, at sea, and in the air. Hitler's ally, Mussolini, felt that this once-Roman sea should, after twenty centuries, become an Italian-ruled sea again. In 1939, he invaded Albania. In September 1940, he launched an attack against British-held Egypt from the Italian colony of Libya, and two months later he decided to attack Greece. Envious of the success of his German ally in Western Europe, the Italian dictator wanted to show that he too was capable of opposing the British, and conquering an empire as the Roman Caesars had in ancient times.

However, Italy was poorly prepared for war. The morale of its soldiers was low. Officers showed little enthusiasm, for many would have preferred not to have joined in the conflict on the side of the Germans. Italian weapons were mediocre and they had few tanks and planes. Mussolini's army was not up to the ambitions of its commander.

At the beginning of 1941, crushed by the British navy's bombardments, machine-gunned by the fighter planes of the Royal Air Force, and surrounded by British tanks, the Italians were defeated in Libya. Only German reinforcements from Rommel's *Afrikakorps* saved them from total disaster.

The situation was not much better in Greece two months later. The Italian action also turned out a total failure. Not content with having repelled the enemy, the Greeks penetrated Italian-occupied Albania.

Hitler, who was preparing operation 'Barbarossa', was worried. His plans were threatened by the collapse of his Italian ally. In order to rescue her, he decided to intervene in the Balkans. On 2 March, a German army was established in Bulgaria with the consent of the king. At the end of the month, Yugoslavia was seized after ten days of lightning war. Greece now became an easy target. The Germans took control within a few weeks. From 20 to 31 May, German paratroopers completed these conquests by taking possession of Crete after the first large-scale airborne operation in history. Despite enormous losses, 20,000 paratroopers ran the British off the island.

In Libya, the desert war was developing. It took the form of numerous offensives and counteroffensives in which the Germans, commanded by Rommel, fought against British troops, who were supported by Canadians, Australians, New Zealanders, Indians, and Free French. The entire British Empire participated in the defence of Egypt. The battlefield for this strange war was a sun-scorched desert of sand and rocks.

The desert terrain was ideal for mechanized vehicles and mobile equipment. The adversaries confronted each other in tank attacks and artillery duels. During the summer of 1942, Rommel's skill and power overcame the British. He occupied Tobruk, and crossed the Egyptian border, leaving the road to Alexandria and Cairo wide open. The only obstacle was the small coastal town of El Alamein where the British had set up a solid

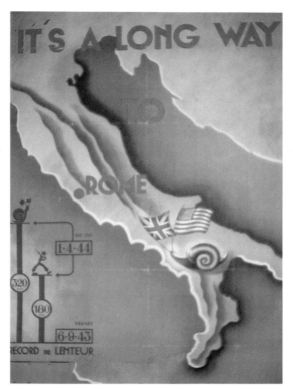

line of defence. However, Rommel and his troops were exhausted after months of fighting, and their equipment was worn out. They were not to go any further. El Alamein held out and in November 1942 the British under Field Marshal Montgomery took the initiative. After a long and gruelling battle, Rommel was forced to retreat. Gradually he pulled back all the way to Tunisia. North Africa was lost for the Germans, particularly as the British and Americans had landed in Morocco and Algeria, from where they threatened Italy.

Having landed in Sicily without heavy losses in July 1943, the Allies forced Italy to surrender on 3 September. Two months earlier, Mussolini had been overthrown by the Grand Fascist Council and placed under house arrest. He was rescued by the Germans who established a line of defence north of Naples against the Allied advance from the South. During the winter of 1943–44, the British, Americans, and Free French now advanced at a snail's pace (as this German poster indicates) in the Abruzzese Mountains. Rome was not liberated until 4 June 1944. Behind the German lines, Italian resistance was active. It attacked German convoys causing heavy losses. Strikes paralysed the country. A Liberation Committee recognized by the Allies took power in the north of Italy, while Mussolini tried to create a Fascist republic in the small town of Salo, near Verona.

From 29 May 1942, the Germans compelled the Jews to wear a yellow star sewn to their clothes. Jews had to obtain this badge by paying with one fabric point from their ration card. In the summer of 1942, Jews began to be rounded up by the thousand and deported to Germany. In the picture on the right, Victor Faynzylber, a veteran from the First World War who was disabled and decorated with the Military Cross, poses with his two children. Only his six-year-old daughter is wearing the star. Mr Faynzylber was to be deported and never returned from the camps. Whereas in France the government let the Germans do as they wished and helped them (they even went so far as to place the French police force at the Germans' disposal), in other countries the rulers protested. For example, the King of Denmark, Christian X, organized the evacuation of Jews living in Denmark to neutral Sweden and began wearing the yellow star himself as a sign of solidarity.

Under Nazi Rule

The footsteps of soldiers dressed in green and grey uniforms pounded in the streets. Huge red flags with the black swastika flapped in the air. In Paris, Brussels, Kiev, Warsaw or Copenhagen, the sight was the same. The Nazi boot crushed Europe wherever it left its mark.

Hitler made arrangements for each 'race', based on the supposed characteristics of that race. Poles and Russians living in Eastern Europe, the key area of the future German 'living space', were to be reduced to slavery so that in two or three generations they would be so weak that they would cease to exist. The French would be entitled to live. They would farm the land to feed Germany, which was the only country intended for industry. The French were to produce wine and cognac, dresses and perfume which the Germans valued highly. As for the Scandinavians, who were considered closely related to the German people, they would be assimilated little by little.

But before the Führer could build this new Europe of his dreams, he had to win the war. The fate of territories conquered by Germany was decided according to the needs of the conflict. Poland disappeared from the map. Part of it was simply annexed to the 'Great Reich', the rest was under the rule of a 'General Government' directly dependent on Berlin.

The war, which was supposed to have been over in a flash, turned out to be longer than expected. It ate up men and equipment. More and more planes, tanks, and ammunition had to be produced. A gigantic army had to be fed and clothed. The German economy could not keep pace. So the Reich pillaged the occupied countries. France, for instance, had to pay outrageous sums: 300 million francs per day in November 1942! Moreover, hundreds of convoys of wheat, meat, iron, and aluminium were sent to Germany. Poles, Frenchmen, Greeks, and Belgians went hungry, and in the winter they suffered dreadfully from the cold.

From 1941, everything was rationed in France. Coupons were needed for bread, meat, textiles, and soap. Substitutes called 'ersatz' appeared. Saccharin replaced sugar, and chicory was used instead of coffee. A substitute for soap was made from horse chestnut flour or alfalfa roots. Newspapers gave recipes on how to make mayonnaise

without eggs or oil, or talked about new foods, such as thistles whose 'young tender roots may be used for human consumption either raw, peeled, or grated and prepared like carrots, or cooked like a root vegetable'. Jerusalem artichokes and swedes, which before the war had been used as animal feed, often appeared on tables.

In Europe's large cities, finding food was so difficult that people had to resort to illegal buying and selling — called the 'black market'. In the countryside, food was not in such short supply and some farmers sold their surplus products at a high profit to dealers or hungry city dwellers.

The Nazis were not satisfied with pillaging the countries they occupied. They needed manpower. Beginning in 1939 in Poland and Czechoslovakia, and moving in 1941 to Yugoslavia and the USSR, workers were rounded up in factories and on the streets and immediately sent to Germany to provide the Reich with labour. In France, Belgium, and Holland, the occupiers first called for volunteers, with no response. In agreement with the German authorities, Laval adopted the system of 'relief': for every three French volunteers, one prisoner of war would be sent home. It was a failure, and in 1942, France was placed under a system of compulsory work service. In the beginning, people were greatly taken by surprise, and

If the black market was a crime, as this poster said, how many Frenchmen were criminals? In a country which had to supply enormous quantities of food and equipment to the victors, even German companies bought things on the black market. Wine was exchanged for ham, geese for a radio set, cigarettes for cloth. The repression severely affected the less well-off. A search of passengers on an average train would have revealed enough in their baggage to send them to prison for several months! But such restrictions did not really exist for those who had enough money.

few were able to avoid being drafted for work. By 1943, however, young people joined the Resistance thus avoiding transfer to Germany.

The whole of occupied Europe was in the service of Nazi Germany. Almost everyone, whether he or she wanted to or not, had to contribute to the war effort. But some — the gypsies and especially the Jews — met a very different fate, rapid and systematic annihilation.

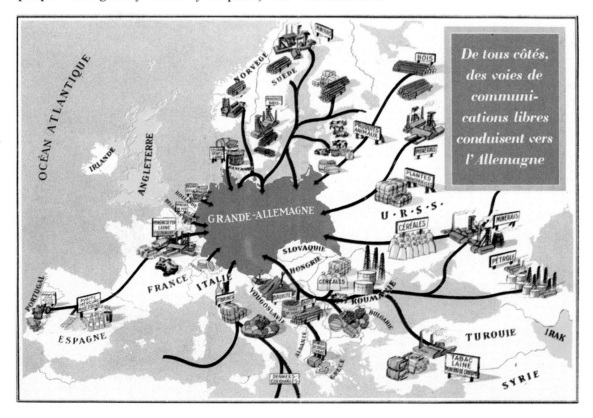

This 1940 German propaganda picture unwittingly illustrates the pillage of Europe by the Third Reich with the phrase 'From all sides free communication routes lead to Germany'.

The Genocide of the Jews

'They are propagators of infection. They spread the plague . . . They poison the gutters. When they arrived in Germany they had nothing except infectious diseases'.

In the mind of Hitler, who pronounced these words in 1938, the Jewish 'virus' had to be eliminated in a war 'like the one waged in the previous century by Pasteur and Koch'. The Jew had to be treated 'like the germ of tuberculosis which could contaminate a healthy body'. Hitler thought that only in this way could Germany and, thanks to its efforts, the rest of the world, become healthy again.

As soon as Poland was occupied, the 3,250,000 Jews living in the country were hunted down, separated from the rest of the population, and packed into ghettos (special areas of towns or cities) such as the one in Warsaw. Living conditions there were particularly atrocious. Every morning the bodies of hundreds who had died in the night from hunger, cold, or typhus were collected.

During the German attack on Russia in June 1941, special detachments called *Einsatzgruppen* accompanied the *Wehrmacht* (the German armed forces). The only task assigned them in the conquered territories was to massacre the Jews. They exterminated 600,000 of them. Very soon, however, their haphazard methods appeared insufficient to Hitler, for he wanted to do away with all the Jews in occupied Europe. A plan for a 'final solution to the Jewish problem' was drawn up on 20 January 1942. New concentration camps were opened that were completely different from those such as Dachau which Hitler had built simply to lock up his opponents. They were extermination camps. They were built on Polish territory, first Chelmno, then Belzec, Sobiba, and Treblinka. The most infamous

In the barracks of the death camps, several people were forced to sleep on one straw mattress. Decimated by the gas chambers, hunger, forced labour, cold, typhus, and general ill-treatment, millions of men, women, and children paid with their lives for the racist theories of the Nazis.

of all these death camps was Auschwitz.

The tragic journeys of Jews, whether Belgian, Polish, French, Greek, Hungarian, or Dutch were all alike. First a census was taken of them. Then they were excluded from all social life. In France, this task was carried out on the initiative of the Vichy government and it was often the French police, upon the order of the Germans, who performed the round-up. In Paris, in the early morning of 16 July 1942, 12,884 people were arrested, mostly women and children, and transported by bus to the Vélodrome d'Hiver. From there they were taken to the camp in Pithiviers, then to the one in Drancy, their last stop before Auschwitz.

In Drancy, the Jews were crammed into boxcars without any food or water. Beginning in the summer of 1942, up to four trains of deported persons arrived each day in the camp of Auschwitz. As soon as they got off the train, those who had survived the atrocious journey were brought before an army doctor who directed them either left or right. The line on the left grouped together the strongest. These were mainly men in the prime of life. They were tattooed with a blue number on their forearm. Dressed in striped pyjamas which made them all look alike but did not protect them from the cold, they joined the ranks of starving slaves used for exhausting excavation work. They were skeletons with bulging wild eyes, and generally did not survive more than three months. Most people (the line on the right), in particular the children and old people, were sent directly to gas chambers. The gas, Zyklon B, took three to five minutes to have its effect. The dead bodies were then stripped of their golden rings and teeth and burned in the ovens of the crematoria.

The most modern techniques were thus used to destroy an entire people. Yet, in the camps and ghettos Jews did resist. In Warsaw on 19 April 1943, the German commander, who had been entrusted with the task of eliminating the Jewish ghetto, battled for three weeks against a rebellion organized by a young Jew, Mordecai Anielewicz. In Treblinka on 2 August, the prisoners comprising the special unit responsible for burning the dead bodies attempted to destroy the crematoria.

Even when Germany's defeat was close at hand, the Nazis continued to deport and gas Jews. Trains carried on arriving at the camps even though there were not enough left for troop transport.

Six million Jews perished in the death camps while international institutions, some politicians, and churches looked on but did nothing to stop the slaughter.

'Everything here has been done to demoralize the deported, make them lose all dignity, lead them to give up their humanity, to become savage beasts. A shaved head, a tattooed number on the left arm, the striped uniform of a prisoner . . . a piece of black bread to be divided into three, a liquid called 'soup', interrupted sleep, continual roll calls, and beatings, beatings without reason, smashing, wounding, deadly beatings. Not a moment of respite, not a minute to breathe, to think, to realize. And the ovens which pour out smoke day and night'.
(Eye-witness account by Henry Bulawko, deported to Auschwitz)

The Resistance

On the night of 31 December 1941, Jean Moulin parachuted into Vichy France. He had left London with the mission of bringing together the various resistance organizations. He achieved this unity in February 1943 when he founded the CNR, or National Council for Resistance, of which he became President. But on 23 June 1943, while holding a meeting on the outskirts of Lyons, Jean Moulin fell into the hands of the Germans. Horribly tortured, he did not speak or give away any name except his own. He died while being transported to Germany.

On 17 June 1940, two German officers went to see Jean Moulin, the Prefect of the department of Eure-et-Loir. They wanted him to sign a document accusing Senegalese soldiers of having killed women and children in the town of Saint-Georges-sur-Yonne. The German army, however, was responsible for the massacre. Jean Moulin refused to sign and was almost beaten to death. He escaped to London where General de Gaulle entrusted him with the mission of unifying French resistance. Moulin was betrayed and ended up in the hands of the Germans in June 1943. He died while being deported.

On 26 June 1940, when the Germans were advancing through Brittany, every man on the island of Sein took to his fishing boat and headed for London to continue the fight.

In the north of France, where the fighting in May and June had left many English soldiers in hiding, Maurice Dechaumont set up a secret network to help them escape.

In the city of Toulouse during the same month, the Jewish militant David Knout typed an appeal to resist and secretly distributed it.

In September in Nantes, Royan, and Rennes, the cables used by the German army to send messages were cut. Pierre Roche, who committed an act of sabatoge in La Rochelle, was sentenced to death and executed.

France was not the only country with a Resistance movement. In all the countries invaded by the German, Italian, and Japanese armies, patriots spontaneously formed groups, refusing to recognize the occupation of their national soil. Sovereigns and governments who did not agree to collaborate went into exile in London. Czechs, Poles, Norwegians, Dutchmen, Belgians, Yugoslavs, and Greeks found refuge in the British capital. These exiles' main task was to spread propaganda and information. Each day the BBC broadcast thirty-five hours of programmes to eighteen occupied European countries. Very rapidly, a wide variety of organizations began to form. In 1942, the Belgian group set up a central network to send mail from Belgium to England.

In March 1942, the Resistance took on a new look. The Germans and Japanese suffered their first setbacks in Russia and in the Pacific, and hope reappeared in the occupied countries. Moreover, many young people preferred to go underground than be forced to work in Germany. Members of the Resistance no longer limited themselves to sabotaging communication routes or

In a farmyard in the Haute Loire, young Resistance recruits learn to use the arms that the British dropped to them by parachute.

44

factories working for the enemy, or to spreading information. Forming a real 'shadow army', they now attacked German soldiers and officers, and even went so far as to assassinate Nazi leaders such as Reinhard Heydrich, killed in Prague by Czech resistance fighters on 27 May 1942. In the words of Charles Tillon, the head of the French Francs-Tireurs (snipers) and Partisans, they were as 'elusive as drops of mercury because they were always regrouping themselves'.

While the German losses caused by these guerrilla actions were small compared with those of the major battles, they still played an important role in undermining the morale of the occupying armies, which did not feel safe anywhere. Helped by the policemen of countries whose governments collaborated, the Gestapo and the SS mercilessly tracked down those whom they called terrorists. Once arrested, these people were viciously tortured, deported, or shot. But repression did not prevent membership in the Resistance from continually increasing.

In some European countries, the Resistance assumed considerable proportions. In Yugoslavia the partisans, under the leadership of Marshal Josip Tito, became a real army, equipped, thanks to the British, with a sizeable amount of weapons. In the USSR groups organized by Stalin and the Communist Party built up a feeling of insecurity within the German ranks demoralizing the occupying forces.

The outcome of the war was, of course, determined by the major battles fought by regular armies. Yet the role of the Resistance movement should not be underestimated, for it played an important part in the war. It bore witness especially to the dignity of those who preferred to die on their feet rather than live on their knees.

The red poster

Many immigrants gave their lives for the liberation of France. In February 1944, the Germans covered walls with this red poster which stated 'Liberators? Liberation by the army of crime', and portrayed twenty-three resistance fighters as if they were common criminals. They were sentenced to death and executed.

As soon as he arrived in London, de Gaulle created units to fight alongside the British. They were the FFL, or Free French Forces. Between 27 May and 1 June 1942, in the middle of the Libyan desert, the FFL commanded by General Marie-Pierre Koenig confronted the Germans for the first time. They inflicted heavy losses on Rommel's troops.

Stalingrad

'The German invaders are heading straight for Stalingrad and the River Volga . . . to fall back would confirm our defeat and be a terrible loss for our homeland. If we continue to retreat, we will be without cereals, without raw materials, without plant or factories, without railways . . . We can't afford another single step backward!'

This message, which Stalin published on 7 September 1942, reflected the seriousness of the situation. Despite the halt forced on the German armed forces outside Leningrad and Moscow, the USSR was in a critical state. In the spring of 1942, the Germans had resumed the offensive and captured new territory in the south and west.

Among the goals set by Hitler for his troops was Stalingrad (now called Volgograd). The city, which spread over 40 kilometres (25 miles) along the right bank of the River Volga, was an industrial centre of 800,000 inhabitants and a major port. To take Stalingrad would mean cutting the USSR in two and depriving the country of the Volga, the immense waterway which linked the north of the Soviet Union to the south. It would also mean winning a psychological victory, for the city had been named after the leader of the USSR.

At the end of August, the offensive launched by the German Sixth Army of General Friedrich Paulus had seemed on the verge of success. His armoured tanks had reached the Volga north of the city, which was in flames due to continual bombing. Stalingrad was being reduced to a heap of rubble. But those defending it formed groups around walls, gutted buildings, cellars, barricades. When the German troops attacked, fierce street battles began. The two sides fought over every building and every street. Sleeping and eating little, the fighting soldiers waged a pitiless war. The battles often ended in hand-to-hand combat, and no prisoners were taken.

By November, the Germans had succeeded in taking control of the centre of the city and began attacking the industrial areas where each factory had been transformed into a fortress. But in this fierce battle which went on for weeks in the cold and snow, Paulus's army began to weaken and suffered increasingly heavy losses.

However, Hitler was obstinate and ordered the offensive to continue. The Germans were not aware that the Soviets were preparing an extraordinary counteroffensive to save Stalingrad and wipe out its besiegers. In absolute secrecy, without any exchange of paper between Moscow and the front, without any written order that might fall into the hands of the enemy, Zhukov brought together 1,000,000 men, 6,000 tanks, and 3,000 planes. He organized his troops like immense pincers ready to close on Paulus's army.

On 18 November 1942, the Soviet plan went into action. Five days later the Germans were surrounded and 300,000 soldiers of the *Wehrmacht* were trapped. Neither the planes of the *Luftwaffe* which tried to resupply them nor the armies sent to rescue them from the grip of the Red Army could save them from defeat. Starved, decimated by the cold,

In this Russian poster, where the word Stalingrad is printed in red, a Soviet soldier strangles a German soldier with a rope symbolizing the River Volga.

Звезда золотая—
    Отчизны награда—

За мужество,
    стойкость
        и мощь Сталинграда:

Он Волгу,
    одетую в льды и снега,

Как петлю,
    набросил
        на шею врага!

Сталинград

р Волга

and without ammunition, the Germans died in their thousands. 'We have eaten the last horses,' General Paulus wrote in his diary. 'Would you ever have imagined soldiers rushing to the old carcass of a horse to cut off its head and devour its raw brain?' On 28 November, a soldier wrote in his diary, 'I'm ready to eat cat meat. I've heard it's not at all bad. The soldiers have turned into corpses or madmen. All they look for is food to put into their mouths. They no longer dive down and take cover at the sound of Russian shells. We don't have the strength to walk or lie down anymore.'

On 24 January 1943, Paulus informed Hitler of the desperate situation. One hundred and fifty thousand of his soldiers had already died. The Führer refused him permission to surrender, but Paulus decided to do so anyway. On 31 January Paulus and his staff were taken into custody by the Soviets. By 2 February the Soviets reported that all German resistance had ceased and 90,000 troops were taken prisoner. Thousands of dead bodies, both of the German attackers and Russian defenders, lay in the fields, in the streets of Stalingrad, and in the cellars. When the order was given to destroy these frozen bodies, they were piled up like firewood in layers separated by railway sleepers and burned.

News of the Soviet victory had a considerable effect all over the world. In Germany, Hitler ordered that there be two days of national mourning. Elsewhere there was renewed hope that Nazism would come to an end. Many people believed that the Soviets had just dealt it a blow from which it could never recover.

From 5 to 17 July 1943, one of the most important battles of the war took place in the region of Kursk. In order to crush the German offensive, the Soviets used the formidable power of their artillery — more than 250 guns per kilometre along the front.

The USSR Counterattacks

Winter 1943–44: The German retreat turned into a rout. Having used up all their fuel, the soldiers of the Wehrmacht *abandoned their artillery, tanks and lorries on the side of the road without even destroying them.*

After its victory in Stalingrad, the Soviet Red Army resumed the offensive. Stalin was now certain of final victory against Nazism. Thanks to the production in his arms factories — wisely located in the east so the German army never reached them — and the supplies sent him by the British and the Americans, he was able to put together an army with equipment superior to that of the Germans.

Hardened by months of fighting, and continually reinforced with fresh troops, the men of the Red Army prepared to free Soviet soil of the German presence. Hitler, who still wanted to believe in a possible collapse of the USSR, was counting on new tanks (the 'Tigers'), modernized artillery, and the bravery of his troops to stop the Russians.

On 12 July 1943, on the plain of Kursk, Germans and Soviets confronted one another in one of the largest tank battles in history. Between them the *Wehrmacht* and the Red Army deployed 3,500 tanks in the battle. The Red Army's fire power was far superior to that of the Germans. In one day of fighting, the Germans lost more than 350 tanks and over 10,000 officers and men. The battle of Kursk was the turning point, and it broke the German army's back. For the Germans, the

eastern front became a gaping abyss in which vast quantities of their reinforcements and war vehicles were swallowed up. In addition to fighting against the Red Army, the Germans had to contend with continual guerrilla action by groups of local partisans who attacked isolated units, sabotaged communication lines, and blew up railway lines and trains. By the end of 1943, only 30 percent of German convoys were reaching their destination.

The Soviet troops also encountered devastation and death as they freed the USSR from the Nazi presence. Each time the Red Army liberated a town, it discovered widescale massacres ordered by the Nazis. On 6 November, it entered Kiev and found in the ravine of Babi Yar one of the largest mass graves of the war. During two years of occupation, the Nazis had executed nearly one hundred thousand individuals, the majority of whom were Jews. But Babi Yar was only one site among thousands where the Red Army found signs of the terrible atrocities committed by Hitler's troops. Little by little, month by month, however, all the major cities of the country were rid of the Germans.

In the spring of 1944, the Red Army crossed the Soviet border. In April it entered Romania, in July Bulgaria and Hungary. In all these countries, Stalin was determined to establish Communist governments friendly to, and dependent upon, the USSR.

In July, the Russian troops entered Poland and reached the River Vistula. In German-occupied Warsaw a rebellion broke out. The Nazis crushed it ruthlessly. On 2 October, the last rebels stopped fighting. The city was a heap of rubble containing 200,000 bodies. The Red Army had not intervened to help the rebels, who obeyed orders from a Polish provisional government set up in London in 1939. Stalin had his own Polish allies whom he wanted to place at the head of the country. For Stalin, refusing to send any help to the rebels in Warsaw was a way of getting rid of future opponents of his planned Soviet grip on Poland.

Soviet pilots celebrate victory after a sortie. Although the Soviet airforce was small at the beginning of the war, it had always had excellent planes and good pilots. In 1943, it succeeded in outclassing the German airforce. In 1944, the USSR produced 30,000 aircraft, and Germany, lacking fuel, had to abandon the control of East European skies to the Soviets.

Men and Machines

The Second World War was not only waged on the battle front. It was also fought behind the lines, in factories. The time was long gone when wars were fought by small armies made up of professional soldiers carrying rifles and dependent for food on the land where they were fighting. This war involved a considerable number of soldiers who used highly sophisticated and costly equipment, which had to be replaced as soon as it was destroyed, worn out, or superceded by new inventions. Fuel was also needed for planes, tanks, and submarines.

When Britain declared war, the British army only had 185,000 soldiers. It rapidly drafted new recruits, and by 1940 there were more than one and a half million. Being short of weapons, instructors trained the new recruits with broom handles. From 1941, almost every man aged between eighteen and fifty-one was mobilized. In December of the same year women began joining the non-combatant, or auxiliary services of the armed forces.

Faced with a war that lasted longer than predicted and took place on several fronts, the *Wehrmacht* was obliged to increase the number of its soldiers. This grew from 5.6 million men in 1940 to 9.5 million in 1943. This increase would obviously not have been possible without the mobilization of ever-younger recruits and the conscription of citizens from regions annexed to the Reich, such as Alsace and Lorraine.

However, arms as well as men were needed to make war. Very quickly Britain mobilized its economy for the war effort, giving priority to the manufacture of planes, ships, and ammunition. From 1939 to 1944, Britain produced 70,000 planes; from 1940 to 1943, it tripled its tonnage of ships launched.

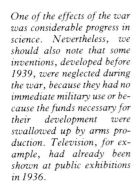

One of the effects of the war was considerable progress in science. Nevertheless, we should also note that some inventions, developed before 1939, were neglected during the war, because they had no immediate military use or because the funds necessary for their development were swallowed up by arms production. Television, for example, had already been shown at public exhibitions in 1936.

PUT MORE PUNCH INTO PRODUCTION

Deprived of part of its territory by the German invasion of June 1941, the Soviet Union quickly reorganized its industry. On Stalin's orders, 1,300 factories were dismantled and transported beyond the Urals where they were rebuilt. Military production was able to supply the army with artillery superior to that of the enemy. The quality of the Soviet equipment was often excellent; the T 34 tank, for example, which the Germans considered to be the best tank of the War.

In Germany, war production increased at an amazing rate. In 1943, the architect Albert Speer, who was already Minister of Equipment and Ammunition, also became responsible for armaments and other areas of war production. He set up such a soundly-based industry that it survived the conflict and enabled Germany, with American aid, to experience a post-war 'economic miracle'. During the last six months of the war, the Germans managed to produce 12,740 fighter planes, whereas they had had only 771 at the outbreak of hostilities in 1939.

A very large labour force was needed for all this industry, but the men were fighting at the front. In Britain, between June 1940 and December 1941, the number of persons employed in war factories increased by two million. The working day was made longer and women were employed on a massive scale.

In Nazi Germany, however, women were required to stay at home and devote their time to the duties of motherhood. Hitler preferred using forced immigrants, prisoners of war, and compulsory labour in the German factories.

Along with war production, countries undertook intensive research programmes to develop new arms. Until 1942, the Allies were the only ones to use secret weapons and techniques, such as radar. But in 1943, faced with the superiority of its enemies, the Germans believed they had to invent a revolutionary new weapon in order to win the war. The Nazi leaders stepped up research efforts. At the end of 1944 these resulted in the use of the first jet fighter, the Messerschmitt Me 262, and of the V1 and V2 rockets, which caused great damage, especially in Britain. The most formidable weapon of war, however, was to come from the United States.

Above left and below: Examples of Allied propaganda posters demanding more production.

COAL is needed for the FACTORIES

GIVE 'EM BOTH BARRELS

The Might of America

'Let nobody say it cannot be done. It must be done and we are prepared to do it'. These words were spoken by President Roosevelt when he presented his 'victory programme' on 6 January 1942. A total of 60,000 planes and 45,000 tanks had to be produced in 1942, and 125,000 planes and 75,000 tanks in the following year.

American war production started slowly in 1940, when the president declared that the United States had to be the arsenal of democracy. It experienced ups and downs in 1941 and 1942, but was in top gear by 1943. The figures speak for themselves: within four years, the United States built 65,000 landing craft, 320,000 pieces of artillery, 15,000,000 small arms, more than 4,000,000 tonnes of ammunition, and more than 1,000,000 lorries. The country also supplied aid to Stalin. This equipment was shipped mostly by way of Iran, at enormous cost. At the end of the Persian Gulf, on the Iranian coast, the Americans built two ports that were linked to Tehran by a 1,100-kilometre (700-mile) long railway. All together the United States supplied 35 percent of the arms used to fight Germany and 86 percent of those used against Japan.

At the beginning of the war, it was easy to find labour to produce these war supplies. Seven to eight million people were unemployed at the time. Little by little, however, unemployment disappeared and labour began to become scarce. The working day became longer. New types of workers were needed, so young people, women, and the elderly went to work in factories. The number of workers increased from forty-six million in 1940 to fifty-three million in 1944. Those living in the countryside moved to towns in order to work in the factories. Blacks left the South for California and for the large cities in the Midwest and the East.

Nevertheless, the need to produce quickly and in large quantities was such that this labour force was still not large enough. The war industry had to change its methods. Assembly line production, where each worker performed only one task in an allotted period of time, was introduced in arms factories. Its effectiveness proved spectacular. A Swedish-designed gun which required 450 hours of work in Sweden could be built in 10 hours in an American factory. In 1941, a shipbuilding yard needed 6 months to launch a liberty ship. Later, a ship could be put to sea every 12 days. At the end of the war, the five enormous factories of the Boeing firm were building six B-29 bombers (referred to as 'flying fortresses') every day. A large number of engineers worked continually to improve them, reducing production costs from $3 million to $600,000 in 1945.

Energy and raw materials for the war effort had to have first priority. Fuel was rationed. To save on cloth, clothes could have only a certain number of pockets, and women's nightdresses could not extend below the knee!

Meanwhile, scientific research was making progress. The Americans were the first to perform open-heart surgery. They industrialized a British invention, penicillin, on such a large scale that those wounded in the war or injured at work were no longer at risk from a generalized infection. In the field of nuclear research, the United States particularly showed its superiority. The Manhattan Project, which eventually resulted in the dropping of the atomic bomb on Hiroshima, mobilized enormous scientific and technical resources.

For Americans, the war was a crusade for freedom and liberty. This poster shows GIs passing in front of the ghosts of soldiers from the War of Independence, 1776–83.

Women replaced men in Boeing factories where B-27 and B-29 bombers were built.

From left to right are General Douglas MacArthur, in charge of operations in the South Pacific; President Franklin Roosevelt; Admiral Chester Nimitz, Commander-in-Chief of the navy and in charge of the North Pacific; and General George C. Marshall, Chief of Staff.

Reconquering the Pacific

The fighting in the Pacific forced soldiers on both sides to adapt to a new type of warfare without precedent in the annals of history. First both sides had to win the war against distances.

Japanese war industry had to rely on convoys of raw materials, such as metals, rubber, and copper, from Japanese-occupied territories. The sea routes of these convoys were essential to the continuation of the war and necessary to meet the country's food needs. They had to be protected from American submarines, planes, and ships. American ships, however, first had to cross some of the longest distances ever imposed on warships and merchant vessels. All military equipment, reinforcements, planes, supplies, ammunition, and vehicles left Californian ports. They tooks several weeks to reach Australia, or the islands that were gradually won back from the Japanese.

In this war of endurance, where economic strength counted as much as human courage,

Japan was beaten before it began. Its industrial maximum output did not reach a tenth of that of the United States. In 1943, for instance, Japanese steel production was only 7,800,000 tonnes, whereas that of the United States exceeded 90,000,000 tonnes.

The United States' technological and industrial strength was clearly evident during fighting over the Solomon Islands, east of New Guinea. In this long battle, which lasted from summer 1942 to the beginning of 1944, the Americans gradually showed their superiority. Month after month, the ever-growing number of increasingly modern planes and ships ensured an American victory. Sophisticated radar and anti-aircraft guns on their vessels enabled the Americans to fight the Japanese airforce effectively and outclass its planes. Within a few months, the Japanese lost more than 2,700 planes, including that of Admiral Yamamoto which disappeared into the sea on 17 April 1943.

As the islands and archipelagos held by the Japanese were reconquered, the Americans came up against increasingly fierce resistance. During the summer of 1944, at the time of the American assault on the Marianas Islands, Japanese soldiers fought to the death, preferring suicide to surrender. The reconquest of the Philippines, completed in April 1945, was just as deadly for the Allies, especially as the Japanese used suicide planes for the first time. These were light planes loaded with bombs and flown by volunteers. The kamikaze pilots (as they were called) deliberately crashed their planes into American ships. These sacrifices, which complied with the ancient code of honour of the samurai, known as the Bushido, increased in the last phase of the war.

The Bushido was followed on land in the same way as in the air. In February 1945, while the Americans were capturing the small island of Iwo Jima, Japanese soldiers carrying explosives around their belts threw

themselves against the enemy's command posts or under planes on the ground.

During the summer of 1945, the Americans were engaged in one of the bloodiest and most difficult battles of the entire Pacific war. They were fighting on Okinawa and had to blow up the enemy's blockhouses one by one. Bulldozers had to be used to cover the openings from which Japanese survivors continued to shoot at them. The island was right next to Japan and resistance assumed fanatical proportions. Very few soldiers agreed to lay down their arms, preferring suicide to the dishonour of defeat. After three months of continual fighting, over 100,000 Japanese were dead, including 7,000 kamikazes. American losses totalled 12,000. The incredible death toll of the battles alarmed the American commanders. They dreaded the carnage that would result from an attempt to conquer the Japanese archipelago, where sixty million inhabitants were preparing to fight to protect the sacred ground of their homeland.

American marines have conquered the beach on a Pacific island after their ships' planes and artillery have bombarded Japanese positions. They are unloading food and ammunition. After 'cleaning up' the centre of the island, the troops will set off again to attack another atoll. MacArthur intended to reconquer the entire Pacific with this 'flea jumping' technique. Nimitz preferred proceeding as rapidly as possible with the least casualties. He formed 'task forces' which were independent fighting units. In the centre, aircraft carriers, protected by their squadron and supplied with fuel by cargo ships, launched their planes against specific targets. They prepared the way for the destructive work of the 'flying fortresses' which took off from airfields set up on islands captured from the Japanese. American victories owed as much to the organization of the operations as to the courage of the men; logistics had become the major factor in battles.

The Normandy Landings

Off the coast of Arromanches, a man-made harbour was built. Old boats were tugged along and sunk to form a breakwater. Between this dam and the coast, floating wharves and piers were set up. In less than two months, two million men and 2,000,000 tonnes of equipment were transported to the coast of Normandy.

Grey clouds had been hanging over the coast of Normandy for several days. The sea was rough and the weather so gloomy that the German command was relaxed; an Allied landing was unthinkable. Most of those in charge were not even at their posts. Marshal Rommel, who commanded the Normandy sector, was at a meeting with Hitler, and Field Marshal Karl von Rundstedt was away from the coast.

However, on the night of 5 June 1944, a seemingly endless line of convoys set off across the English Channel towards the French coast. 'D-day' had arrived, and Operation Overlord (the code name given to the Allied landings on the Normandy coast) had just begun.

The task ahead was far from easy. In 1942–43, on an order from Hitler, a chain of fortifications designed by the German engineer Fritz Todt had been built along the entire length of Europe's western coast, from Denmark to the Spanish border. Its purpose was to repel any Allied landing. The coast was protected by an 'Atlantic Wall', made up of guns and blockhouses, and defended by countless submarines. Furthermore, at low tide, the beaches were strewn with giant concrete teeth or wooden tripods equipped with detonators.

The Allies knew they had to break through these defences at all costs. The preparation of Operation Overlord was entrusted to General Dwight D. Eisenhower, while the British Field Marshal Bernard Montgomery had the task of co-ordinating the movements of all the Allied forces. In Britain, three million soldiers, mainly British, Canadian, and American, were prepared for the invasion. Shipyards, sometimes specially built for the purpose, turned out thousands of boats. In order to thwart the German defences on the coast, the British Admiral Louis Mountbatten had had the idea of building artificial harbours which could be towed across the channel in sections and assembled on the beaches, one off Vierville and the other off Arromanches. These harbours would enable 40,000 tonnes of equipment and 6,500 vehicles to be unloaded each week. Fuel would be supplied by pipelines laid across the seabed.

In order for the operation to work, the Germans obviously had to be unaware of what was going on. They had to be led to believe that the operations in Normandy were only a diversion. The strength of the

German army, even after five years of war and terrible losses on the eastern front, was far from being destroyed. Between Holland and Spain, they had over sixty divisions. Among these were ten armoured divisions whose tanks, the Panthers and Tigers, were superior to the Allies' Shermans. In order to prevent these armoured divisions from reaching Normandy, the Allies made plans to bomb railways and involve the French Resistance in guerrilla actions.

On the night of 5 June, while the long procession of 5,339 vessels silently made its way across the English Channel, the first of the 10,500 American and British bombers dropped their bombs over the Normandy coast. Thirty-one thousand participated in the operation which lasted from midnight till dawn. Meanwhile, frogmen cut the barbed wire that the Germans had laid in the sea. At 2.00 a.m., 27,000 men, with blackened faces, pockets filled with ammunition, and weapons and grenades strapped to their bodies, were parachuted along the coast. At 6.30 a.m., the first assault troops and tanks landed on the Juno, Gold, and Sword beaches, which were British code names, and the Utah and Omaha beaches, which were the names given by the Americans. Everything went almost as planned. On Omaha beach a strong current carried away small boats, and German resistance was stubborn. Losses were heavy. But eventually, in Sainte-Mère-Eglise, Colonel Krause raised the Stars and Stripes over the door of the town hall.

At the close of the 'longest day', ten divisions with arms and supplies had landed. The British captured Bayeux and on 8 June they met up with the Americans. The liberation of Western Europe had begun.

In order to protect the landings, barrage balloons ('sausages') were attached to warships and equipped with explosives to prevent enemy planes from dive bombing. Within a few days, and despite terrible difficulties, the Normandy landing established a beachhead from which the reconquest of Western Europe was to begin.

General de Gaulle, who was at the head of the French provisional government, landed on a Normandy beach on 8 June. He followed the progress of the Allies while asserting his role as the uncontested head of a liberated France.

From Normandy to Yalta

After the Allied landings in Normandy, the Germans, like the French in 1940, experienced the humiliation of defeat. Within several weeks, the *Wehrmacht* had to abandon Brittany, and a large part of northwestern France. More than 500,000 German soldiers were killed, wounded or taken prisoner. Travelling across the battlefields of the Falaise region, General Eisenhower found, as he later wrote in his autobiography, that roads, paths, and fields were littered with wrecked equipment and the dead bodies of men and animals. It was possible to walk hundreds of yards without stopping and tread only on dead or rotting flesh.

On 15 August 1944, the Allies made another opening in the German defences by landing in the south of France. One month later this army joined up in Burgundy with the army that had landed on the coast of Normandy on 6 June. Throughout all this fighting, the French Resistance helped the Allies along their way. They supplied information, harassed the German troops, and liberated dozens of towns. The Germans sometimes reacted with terrible violence by attacking the civilian population. On 10 June 1944, German soldiers massacred the inhabitants of Oradour-sur-Glane, a quiet village in the region of Limousin. The men were shot; the women and children, shut up in the village church which was then set on fire by the SS, were cut to pieces by a hail of bullets. As they left, the murderers looted and burned down all the houses. They left behind them 642 bodies.

But neither Nazi barbarism nor rearguard fighting by a demoralized army could halt the Allies' progress and the liberation of occupied territory. All the major French cities and most of the surrounding countryside were gradually freed from the German presence. On 19 August 1944, Paris rebelled and rid itself of the Nazis with the help of the second armoured division of the Free French Forces under General Leclerc, and the Americans.

In the liberated regions, collaborators and notorious Pétain supporters were arrested and sometimes executed after summary trials. This 'weeding out' was applied, often without distinction, not only to traitors and torturers working for the Gestapo during the occupation, but also to men and women guilty simply of liking Marshal Pétain.

During the summer of 1944, when the German western front was splitting at the seams and the Russians were advancing rapidly in the east, a plot was being prepared in Germany. To dozens of generals, senior officers, and even ordinary members of the Nazi party, Hitler had become a danger to their country. The conspirators believed that the Führer was leading Germany to a terrible disaster by obstinately wanting to continue a war already lost. But the attempt to assassinate Hitler with a bomb on 20 July 1944 failed, and over 5,000 people, accused by Hitler of being involved in the plot, were arrested and executed. Hitler declared on the radio that, 'The guardian angel which saved me from all evil tells me that I must continue my work towards victory. I will continue.' Thus began several months of agony for the Third Reich. Everywhere German troops were in retreat, although they sometimes attempted desperate last-minute counteroffensives, such as the attack on the Americans launched in the Ardennes on 16 December 1944. Lacking planes, tanks, and fuel, the German offensive lasted only nine days. Known as the Battle of the Bulge, it was a final attempt to break the Allied circle which was tightening on Germany.

For the Allies, total victory against the

Germans was now certain. Between 2 and 20 February 1945, Churchill and Roosevelt met Stalin at Yalta in the Crimea. During this conference they planned the future, discussed the Soviet Union's entry into the war against Japan, organized the future occupation of Germany, and defined the role of a United Nations Organization whose first meeting was scheduled for 25 April 1945, in San Francisco. This new organization to replace the ill-fated League of Nations would be entrusted with the task of organizing the peace, and preventing war from occurring in future.

During the Allied landings and the fighting that followed, the French Resistance played an important role in delaying the arrival of German help. Railways and railway equipment between the north and Normandy were destroyed. The boiler of this locomotive, sabotaged by the railwaymen of the northern network, has exploded.

On 3 June 1943, General de Gaulle set up the French Committee of National Liberation in Algiers and on 19 August 1943 he became the only French leader recognized by the Allies. In June 1944, he transformed the Committee into the provisional government of the French Republic of which he was elected President. It was on the basis of this that de Gaulle asserted his authority over the liberated territory and the Resistance movements. On 25 August 1944, after his triumphant walk down the Champs-Elysées, he made a speech at the Paris city hall. In this historic building, the Second and Third Republics had been proclaimed in 1848 and 1870.

In the Berlin war museum, damaged by Allied bombs, two guards carry dummies dressed in the Wehrmacht *uniform. This seems a laughable image of the Third Reich, which had founded its power on the force of arms and which was destroyed by bombs. It fell victim to a war it had started, believing itself invincible. Five years were enough to wipe out the Reich that was supposed to last a thousand years.*

The Death of the Third Reich

By the beginning of 1945, the Third Reich was on the verge of collapse. Day and night, British and American planes bombed Germany's cities, reducing them to smoking ruins. Over 600,000 civilians had already been killed in air raids. The hundreds of thousands of men still fighting at the front did not know whether their wives and children were alive or dead. Fleeing from the Soviet advance in the east, over ten million refugees had taken to the roads, sleeping in makeshift shelters, or living in ruins. Food was desperately short.

Road and rail traffic had virtually stopped. Trains and railway lines were bombed regularly. Canals and rivers could not be used. Very few Germans still believed victory was possible, and the number of suicides increased.

However, Hitler and a few Nazi leaders still hoped that the situation would change. The new weapons, the V2 rocket and the Messerschmitt 262, the first jet plane, began to take effect. Submarines fitted with highly sophisticated equipment were being built, and atomic scientists were building a nuclear weapon. But these weapons simply could not be manufactured in time. Hitler also hoped to divide the Allies. Some of his colleagues thought that it would be possible to stop the war against the British and Americans and join with them to fight the Soviets. But the alliance against Nazism was solid, and the Third Reich crumbled.

On the night of 13 February 1945, the city of Dresden suffered the most terrible bombing of the Second World War. Throughout the entire night, successive waves of American bombers rained phosphorous bombs on the city. When they came into contact with the air and the ground, these bombs burst into flames, drowning buildings, streets, and shelters in a sea of fire. Within a few hours, 250,000 people had been wiped out by the fire, either burned to death or asphyxiated.

All the land controlled by the Germans in the east was gradually reconquered. Romania capitulated on 23 August 1944; Bulgaria signed an armistice on 28 October 1944; Poland was liberated at the end of January 1945; and Tito's Yugoslavian partisans chased the last Germans from their soil in April 1945.

Faced with the Allied troops, Hitler threw his last regiments into battle. Beside the soldiers fought twelve-year-old children, adolescents, old people, and women, all of whom had been drafted for combat. But nothing could stop the Allied forces. In the west, the Americans crossed the Rhine on 7 March 1945. In the east, the Russians approached the outskirts of Berlin. On 25 April 1945, the Russian and American troops met on the banks of the River Elbe.

At the end of April, the Russians assembled one million men and 15,000 guns around Berlin. The final assault had begun. Hitler was trapped in his bunker, which had walls over 5 metres (15 feet) thick. He had no hope left. On 30 April, he committed suicide, after handing over power to Admiral

ENTRE LE MARTEAU ...

... ET L'ENCLUME !..

'Between the hammer and the anvil'. This was a typical French poster of the time, depicting the crushing of Nazi Germany by the Allied forces.

Doenitz, who understood that any resistance was now useless.

On 8 May in the French city of Reims, Germany signed an unconditional surrender. The ceremony was repeated the day afterwards in Berlin. The Third Reich, which according to Hitler's promise was to last for a thousand years, was divided and occupied by foreign armies. Its major cities had been destroyed, millions of soldiers and civilians were dead, and countless others were on the way to prisoner-of-war camps.

Russian troops raise the Red flag on top of the Reichstag (parliament building) in Berlin. The capital of the Reich had fallen. The Soviets were determined to enter the city before the British and Americans. Nearly 15,000 guns had poured their fire on a city already battered by bombs, forcing Berliners to hide in their cellars for fifteen days. Resistance was desperate but useless until 2 May 1945, when the 70,000 Germans defending Berlin surrendered.

AP INDICATES AIMING POINT

Hiroshima

After the fall of Okinawa in June 1945, Japan's defeat was no longer in doubt. The country was already partly destroyed by the continual bombings of the 'flying fortresses'. It was exhausted after years of war, and the United States, masters of the Pacific Ocean, set up a merciless blockade. In March 1944, the inhabitants of Tokyo were receiving one piece of fish every five days. The country lacked men. Schoolchildren had to work in factories, and seventeen-year-olds were conscripted. From July 1945, the capital was bombed every day. On 17 and 18 July, six waves of 1,500 bombers destroyed Osaka and Yokohama. Yet, the Japanese people remained fiercely determined. They were prepared for an all-out war on national soil,

even if that meant collective suicide.

After Roosevelt's death in April 1945, Harry S. Truman had become President of the United States. Truman thought that the American army would not be able to invade Japan before 1946 unless it was prepared to sacrifice the lives of a million men. He therefore decided to use a secret weapon, which had been in preparation for years, in order to force the Tokyo government to surrender.

On 16 July, the first experimental atomic bomb had been exploded in the New Mexico desert. President Truman, who was preparing to meet Stalin and Churchill in Potsdam, Germany, received a coded message informing him of the experiment: 'Operation performed this morning. Diagnosis still incomplete but results seem satisfactory and already surpass all hopes.'

After that, plans to drop the first uranium bomb, named Little Boy, accelerated. On 5 August, the bomb was assembled and last-minute details taken care of. The crew of the B-29 Superfortress which was to drop the device saw a film showing the power of the new weapon, and was informed of the existence of radioactivity.

On 6 August 1945, at 8.15 and 17 seconds a.m., the bomb bay of the B-29 opened. Suspended from a parachute, the device descended towards Hiroshima. Fifty-one seconds later, at an altitude of 600 metres (2,000 feet), it exploded. A white cloud in the shape of a gigantic mushroom rose 15,000 metres (50,000 feet) into the sky.

At that time in the morning, people in Hiroshima were busy with their daily occupations. Many were going to work. Suddenly, a blinding flash of light tore through the air. Immediately afterwards, houses swayed and collapsed, burying tens of thousands of people beneath the debris. Many people literally vanished into thin air. Hideously burned and mutilated human beings staggered in the streets, twisted in agony. Everywhere fires broke out spreading from one building to the next. The 12 square kilometres (4.5 square miles) of the city on which 40,000 buildings had stood, were razed to the ground. Only ruins and ashes remained. The atomic bomb had just killed 130,000 people.

But even the survivors were afflicted — with irreversible changes in their blood and horrible ulcerations — and as the days went

by, they began to die of haemorrhages and infections. Others did not show signs of radiation contamination until weeks or sometimes even months later. Men became sterile and women gave birth to deformed babies. Everyone affected lost their hair; most suffered terrible eye damage, and eventually died of leukaemia or cancer.

Three days later, after the USSR had declared war on Japan and attacked Manchuria, a second bomb was dropped on Nagasaki in a similar operation. It killed 35,000 people and wounded 60,000.

On 15 August, Emperor Hirohito finally announced his decision to surrender. The crowd gathered in front of the imperial palace wept.

The war was over, but the relief everyone felt at seeing this six-year conflict finally ended was tarnished by the horror of the new weapon. Its long-term effects on the survivors and even on their descendants were still not well known. What was known was that it caused the destruction of thousands of men, women, and children in terrible suffering.

While the American military and political leaders responsible for using the bomb realized its destructive power, they reasoned that without it the war would have lasted many more months and cost countless more lives on both sides.

After favourable weather conditions had been reported by two planes flying ahead, the B-29 'Enola Gay' (named after the mother of the commander on board) dropped the atomic bomb on Hiroshima. Before the flight, the crew had watched a film taken during the first atomic test in the New Mexico desert. All the nine airmen and four scientists in the plane knew about the terrible weapon they were going to use on Japan.

A victim of Hiroshima afterwards told the following story:'. . . Without any prior warning, an enemy plane appeared all alone very high above our heads. Its silver wings shone brightly in the sun. A woman shouted, "Oh! look, a parachute!" I turned to look in the direction she was pointing and just at that moment a blinding flash of light filled the sky . . . I was thrown flat on the ground and the world immediately began to collapse around me . . . I rubbed my nose and my mouth with my sash. With horror I discovered that the skin of my face had stuck to the cloth! The skin on my hands and arms was also coming off . . .'

Counting the Cost

It is very difficult to calculate, even approximately, the final toll of the losses incurred during the Second World War. However, it has been estimated that around 45 million people were killed – not including the 11 million Chinese victims of the war against Japan – far greater than the losses of the First World War of 1914–18. Many of the dead were not members of the armed forces, but civilians.

The USSR suffered the worst losses of any of the countries involved in the war. It paid for its victory over Nazism with 20 million dead. Germany and Austria lost 6 million people, half of them civilians. Poland lost almost 18 percent of its population – more than 5 million killed of whom 3 million were Jews. Then there were 2 million dead in Japan, 1,700,000 in Yugoslavia, 500,000 from the UK and the same number in France, 600,000 in Greece, 665,000 in Romania, 450,000 in Hungary and 380,000 in Czechoslovakia, plus those killed in Finland, Norway, Sweden, Albania, Bulgaria and the rest of Europe, in Korea and Indochina, and from the USA, Canada, India, Australia and New Zealand. The exact toll will never be known; what is certain is that the Second World War was the most murderous conflict in history.

Material losses were on the same scale as the slaughter.

But in addition to the human losses and material destruction, the moral cost of the war was extremely high. Photographs taken by the liberating Allies revealed to the world the almost unbelievable horror of the extermination camps. Meanwhile, the production and use of the atomic bomb, a weapon capable conceivably of bringing about the destruction of the world, triggered an awesome arms race and heralded a new era of international distrust and uncertainty.

The city of Dresden, in Germany, in April 1945. On the night of 13 February, and again at midday on the 14th, the Allies carried out on Dresden the most destructive bombing raid the world had ever known. In addition to its own population, the city was full of refugees from the fighting in the east, and it is thought that more than 250,000 people were killed in the raid. Dresden, architecturally one of the most beautiful cities in Europe, was not an important communications centre, nor was it a key industrial city; the raid did nothing to shorten the war.

The Nuremberg Trials

The courtroom in Nuremberg. On the left, the accused listen to the list of their crimes.

The British Prime Minister Churchill declared that the Allied powers would pursue the guilty to the farthest corners of the earth and bring them to justice. On 20 November 1945, in the city of Nuremberg where the Nazi party had held its meetings, criminal proceedings started against twenty-one political and military leaders of the Third Reich. For the first time in history, a war was going to end not only with an armistice or surrender. Aware that they were dealing with enemies of civilization, in 1942 the Allies had already begun drawing up a list of all those who would have to answer for their crimes against humanity. For the misdeeds that the Nazis had organized, ordered, or covered up, for the acts of barbarism that they committed, the prosecution invented the notion of 'crime against humanity'. Also a new word was added to the dictionary: genocide. After six months of proceedings, the lives of ten of the accused were spared. Goering, one of the eleven war criminals sentenced to death, committed suicide in order to escape the punishment of hanging. In every country where the Nazis had committed their crimes, leaders who were just as guilty as those in Nuremberg, but less famous, were tried before courts. They were officers who ordered men, women, and children to be machine-gunned or burned alive. They were the brutal murderers of the concentration camps, or Nazis collaborators who, like the militiamen in France, did the dirty work. Meanwhile, Japanese war criminals were also being brought to justice. But some major Nazi criminals escaped the law. Several found refuge in South and Latin America, using secret networks set up when the war started to turn against the Nazis. In 1960, Adolf Eichmann, who was one of the people mainly responsible for the genocide of Jews, was kidnapped in Buenos Aires, Argentina, by the Israeli secret service and taken to Israel. He was tried before a court in Jerusalem and sentenced to death. Since 1968, international law has declared that people can be prosecuted for crimes against humanity, however long ago the crimes were committed. Time cannot erase these crimes, nor exempt their perpetrators from appearing before the law.

Some Second World War Biographies

Charles de Gaulle

De Gaulle was born in Lille, France, in 1890 into a family of minor Catholic aristocrats. From a very early age, he devoted himself to a military career, and entered the military academy of Saint-Cyr. After the First World War, he published three books in which he spoke out in favour of war being waged by professional armies equipped with tanks.

During the German offensive in May and June 1940, the armoured division commanded by de Gaulle fought bravely and inflicted serious losses on the enemy. He was promoted to the rank of general and brought into the government as Under-Secretary of State for Defence and War. When the armistice was announced on 17 June, de Gaulle flew to London to become Organizer of Free France and head of the provisional government of the French Republic. He resigned in January 1946, feeling that the new French constitution did not enable him to govern. He withdrew to his estate in Colombey-les-Deux-Eglises.

In 1958, he was recalled to office, and launched the Fifth Republic. He granted independence to France's colonies in Africa, put an end to the war in Algeria, and dealt with the crisis caused by the student movement of May 1968. In 1969, the French refused to accept the reforms he proposed. He resigned and retired for good to Colombey, where he died in 1970.

Winston Churchill

Winston Churchill was born in 1874 at Blenheim Palace, near Oxford, into a famous aristocratic family. A descendant of the brilliant general, the Duke of Marlborough, Churchill began his career in the army, fighting on the Indian frontier, in Sudan, and in South Africa. After making a name for himself as a war correspondent during the Boer War, he entered politics in 1900 and soon became a Cabinet Minister in the Liberal government. In 1916 he rejoined the army and fought on the western front. Between the wars he resumed his political career, but found himself increasingly at odds with the government over its policy of appeasement towards the Fascist dictators.

Time and again Churchill warned the western democracies of Hitler's true intentions. Therefore, when war eventually came, it was to Churchill that the British nation turned to lead them. His fierce determination and stirring speeches soon became legendary; more than anyone else he held Britain together when it stood alone against the might of the Nazis.

Churchill was defeated in the general election which followed victory in Europe in 1945, and he became leader of the Conservative opposition. He served his final term as Prime Minister between 1951 and 1955 before age and ill-health forced him to retire, allowing him to concentrate on his writing and painting. When he died in 1965, Britain and the entire world paid tribute to this great and distinguished man.

Franklin Delano Roosevelt

In 1940, for the first time in the history of the United States, a president was elected for a third term of office. Born in 1882 into a wealthy family of Dutch origin, Franklin Roosevelt attended the best schools. He was elected Senator to the New York State Legislature as a Democrat. In 1921 he contracted polio and was left handicapped for the rest of his life. He was governor of the state of New York from 1929 to 1933. Roosevelt did not accept the inevitability of the economic crisis, and he entered the presidential race with a programme to transform the country's economy. He called it the 'New Deal'.

Roosevelt was a convinced enemy of Nazism and Fascism, and at the outbreak of the war he wanted to help the democratic countries. After Pearl Harbor, the entire nation followed him into the all-out war against Germany, Italy, and Japan. He was inflexible towards Nazism, conciliatory with Stalin, and rather hostile to de Gaulle whom he did not like at all. In November 1944, he was re-elected for a fourth term. He died on 2 April 1945, too soon to experience the Allied victory.

President Roosevelt in 1942

Joseph Stalin

The son of a poor cobbler in the small Georgian town of Didi-lilo, Joseph Djugashvili was born in 1879. He went to a religious school and entered a seminary to become a priest, but his revolutionary ideas resulted in his being expelled. He then became a militant socialist, was arrested several times, and deported to Siberia. In 1913, he chose the revolutionary name of 'Stalin', which in Russian means 'man of steel'. After the revolution of 1917, he became Commissar for the Nationalities. Lenin then entrusted him with the office of Secretary to the Communist Party. Ambitious and brutal, after the death of Lenin in 1924, Stalin succeeded in eliminating most of his opponents. By 1929, he was the absolute ruler of the USSR and he governed by terror. After the German invasion, he personified the fight of the Soviets in the 'great patriotic war'. After the war, official historians portrayed Stalin as the only person responsible for victory. While the 'iron curtain' isolated the communist world, the 'friendly guide' and 'father of the people' was the subject of a cult in his country and among

Stalin in uniform in 1950

Communist Party members in other countries. When he died in March 1952, his embalmed body was placed next to Lenin's in the mausoleum of Red Square. In 1956, however, at the Twentieth Congress of the Communist Party of the USSR, Khrushchev denounced Stalin's crimes, condemned his 'personality cult', and prepared the way for 'destalinization'. Stalingrad became Volgograd, and in 1961 Stalin's body was removed from the mausoleum. 67

Mussolini in 1940

Benito Mussolini

Mussolini was born in 1883 in the village of Predappio, in the Romagna district of central Italy. His father was a blacksmith and his mother a teacher. Socialist and pacifist before the First World War, he rapidly changed his views and actively campaigned for Italy's entry into the war. Wounded and much changed by the war, he returned to civilian life.

After the First World War, the economic situation in Italy was disastrous. Mussolini formed around himself a large group of dissatisfied men who comprised the 'Italian fighting fasces' (or *I fascii*) and opposed left-wing militants.

His black-shirted followers soon became known the world over simply as Fascists. Yielding to a largely fictitious 'march on Rome' by tens of thousands of Fascists, King Victor Emmanuel III called Mussolini to power in October 1922.

Within three years, Italy became a dictatorship. All political parties were outlawed, and power was concentrated in the hands of a single party. Its members held all government offices and blindly obeyed their Duce (leader). The regime's motto became: 'Believe, obey, fight'. Skilful propaganda helped Mussolini to retain his hold over the people. He dreamed of restoring to Italy the grandeur of the ancient Roman Empire. He went to war to conquer Ethiopia, supported Franco in Spain, and allied himself with Hitler. On the evening of 24 July 1943, Mussolini was outvoted at the Grand Fascist Council. He was placed under arrest and imprisoned on the order of the king, who wanted to make peace with the Allies. Mussolini was rescued by a German SS commando operation, and set up a Fascist Republic in the north of Italy. In the spring of 1945, he attempted to escape to the Tyrol in the Alps, where he hoped to find refuge. He was captured by a group of partisans and executed. His body was hung up by the feet and exposed to the abuse of the people.

Hirohito

Emperor Hirohito in 1980

Hirohito was born in 1901. According to Japanese tradition, he is the 124th descendant of the sun goddess. Upon the death of his father on 25 December 1926, he ascended the throne of the Empire of the Rising Sun and chose to reign under the name of Showa or 'Illuminated Peace'. Though head of the government and chief of the armed forces, he very quickly left the running of the country to the military leaders who drew Japan into war. Realising that defeat was inevitable, in 1944 Hirohito attempted in vain to put an end to the conflict but was not able to prevent his country from running into catastrophe. After the atomic bomb was dropped on Hiroshima, he made his first radio broadcast, announcing his country's surrender. Despite the defeat, the 1947 Japanese constitution recognized him as sovereign, but his political power was reduced. He is now more of a symbol of a thousand-year-old tradition and a great civilization than the real leader of a country which has become one of the richest in the world today.

Adolf Hitler

For twelve years the fate of Germany was embodied in its Führer, Adolf Hitler. Son of an Austrian customs official, he was born in 1889 in the small town of Braunau-am-Inn on the German border. At the age of eighteen, he was already an orphan but his father had left him with a small inheritance. He left for Vienna where he dreamed of becoming a famous painter, but he failed the entrance exam to the Academy of Fine Arts. When the First World War broke out, he enlisted in the German army and participated in the fighting on the western front. While there, he was wounded and decorated with the Iron Cross.

After the First World War, Hitler moved to Munich where he joined a small nationalist party, the German Workers' National Socialist Party, and became its

Hitler in 1941

President in 1921. In November 1923, an unsuccessful attempt to overthrow the ruling party in Munich resulted in his being sentenced to five years'

imprisonment in the fortress of Landsberg. He only served thirteen months of the sentence but this was enough time for him to write his famous book *Mein Kampf (My Struggle)*. In this embroidered story of his life, Hitler reveals his racist doctrine, his nationalism, and his hatred for democracy. The work soon became the Nazis' bible.

When he was set free, Hitler devoted his time to strengthening his party, which within a few years became a sizeable force. Appointed Chancellor of Germany in 1933, Hitler set up a Nazi regime, and declared himself Führer of the Reich when the elderly president Paul von Hindenburg died. Germany's fate was then linked to that of its ruler. On 30 April 1945, in a Berlin invaded by the Red Army and in ruins, Hitler committed suicide.

Henri Philippe Pétain

Pétain was born in 1856 into a family of farmers in Cauchy-à-la-Tour in the department of Pas-de-Calais in northern France. Philippe Pétain chose a military career. When the First World War broke out in 1914, he was on the verge of retiring as a colonel. Promoted to the rank of army general, he was entrusted on 26 February 1917, with the mission of holding the front at Verdun, where he succeeded in breaking the German offensive. He was admired by his men, whom he tried to spare from sufferings but whom he

mercilessly punished for mutiny. He became a national hero and was named Marshal of France on 19 November 1918.

Certain right-wing extremists wanted to make Pétain a dictator, but he remained faithful to the institutions of the Third Republic. He was Minister of War in 1934, and in 1939 he was France's first ambassador to Franco's Spain. He became Vice-President of the Council under the administration of Paul Reynaud on 18 May 1940.

On 17 June 1940, Pétain was called on by the President of the Republic to head the government, and on 10 July he

was entrusted with the power to transform the country's institutions. He put an end to the Republic and replaced it by the French State, placing himself at the head. On 20 August 1944, the Germans persuaded him to flee and set him up in the castle of Sigmaringen in Bavaria. In the following year, he turned himself over to the French authorities. Brought before the High Court for collaboration with the enemy, he was sentenced to death and national shame. His sentence was commuted to life imprisonment by de Gaulle, and he died on the island of Yeu in 1951 after six years of captivity.

Important dates

January 1933
> Adolf Hitler becomes Chancellor of the German Reich

July 1937
> Japan attacks China

July 1936–March 1939
> Spanish Civil War

29–30 September 1938
> Munich Agreement

1939 August: German- Soviet pact
1 September: German troops enter Poland
2 September: France and Britain declare war against Germany

1940 April: Germany invades Denmark and Norway
10 May: The *Wehrmacht* attacks Western Europe
22 June: France signs armistice with the Third Reich
August–October: Battle of Britain

1941 March: *Afrikakorps* in Libya
22 June: Germany attacks the USSR
7 December: Japan attacks the American base of Pearl Harbour in the Hawaiian Islands
11 December: Germany and Italy declare war on the United States

1942 January–May: Japanese conquests in the Pacific
4–7 June: American air and sea victory at Midway
October: Battle of El Alamein
8 November: Allied landing in North Africa

1943 February: Defeat of the German Sixth Army in Stalingrad
July: Battle of Kursk
9 July: Allies land in Sicily
3 September: Italy signs armistice with Allies

1944 6 June: Allied landings in Normandy, D-Day
15 August: Allied landings in the south of France
25 August: American landings in the Philippines

1945 4–11 February: Yalta Conference
March: Allies cross the Rhine
30 April: Hitler commits suicide
8 May: Germany surrenders
6 August: Atomic bomb dropped on Hiroshima
15 August: Surrender of Japan

Europe in 1955

Member countries of NATO
Neutral countries
Member countries of the Warsaw Pact
- - - - - Borders in 1955
- - - - Borders after 1920

0   200   400   600km

IRELAND
Dublin
GREAT BRITAIN
London
NETHER
Th
Brussels
BELGIUM
Paris
FRANCE
SW
PORTUGAL
Madrid
Lisbon
SPAIN

Imprimé en Belgique par Casterman, s.a., Tournai.   Dépôt légal: avril 1985, D. 1985/0053/117. Déposé au Ministère de la Justice, Paris (loi n° 49.956 du 16 juillet 1949 sur les publications destinées à la jeunesse).

NORWAY

FINLAND

Helsinki

SWEDEN

Oslo

Stockholm

ENMARK

Copenhagen

Danzig

Berlin

EAST GERMANY

Warsaw

RMANY

Prague

POLAND

CZECHOSLAVAKIA

Vienna

AUSTRIA

Budapest

HUNGARY

ROMANIA

Belgrade

Bucharest

YUGOSLAVIA

ITALY

BULGARIA

Sofia

ome

ALBANIA

Tirana

GREECE

Moscow

USSR

Ankara

TURKEY

Publishers' note

On the map, Albania should
have been shown as a
member country of the
Warsaw Pact in 1955.
Albania withdrew from the
Pact in 1968.

Glossary

Alliance   A group of countries united in a common cause
Allies   The group of countries that fought against Germany, Italy, and Japan in the Second World War
Annexation   The act of adding territory to a nation

Collaborate   To co-operate with or aid your country's enemies
Communism   A system of government in which most property and means of production are owned by the state and private ownership is abolished
Conscription   Compulsory joining of the armed forces

Dictator   Someone who has absolute power of rule in a country

Ersatz   An artificial and usually inferior substitute

Genocide   The deliberate extermination of a group of people belonging to a specific culture or religion

Ghetto   An area of a city in which people belonging to one race or nationality live

Pacifist   A person who is against war and believes that peaceful methods should be used to end or solve conflicts
Partisans   Those who engage in harrassment and sabotage of the enemy
Propaganda   Information spread to improve one's own cause or undermine the enemy's cause

Radical   Someone who advocates or supports extreme changes or reforms
Rationing   A situation when goods, such as food, are distributed in limited amounts
Reich   The German word for 'empire'
Resistance   The group of people in an occupied nation who organize secretly to fight for their country's freedom

Socialism   An economic system in which means of production, distribution and exchange are collectively owned by the Community, usually through the State

---

Index